IMAGES
of America

WEST VALLEY CITY

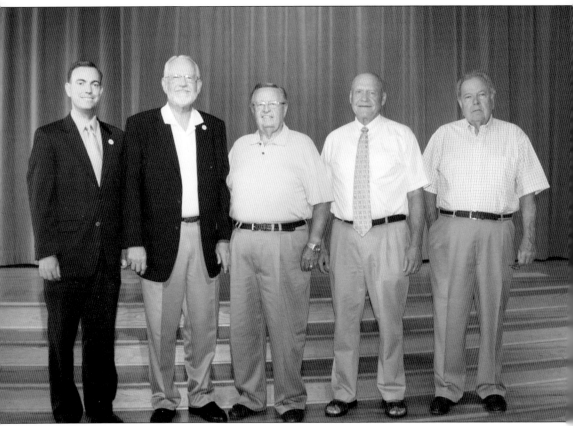

On July 28, 2010, present and former elected officials gathered for a luncheon to celebrate the 30th anniversary of West Valley City's incorporation. All of the living mayors of the city were photographed at this event. The mayors are, from left to right, Mike Winder (2010–present), Dennis Nordfelt (2002–2010), Brent Anderson (1987–1994), Michael Embley (1986–1987), and Gerald Maloney (1982–1986). Henry "Hank" Price (1980–1982) and Gerald Wright (1994–2002) were deceased. (Courtesy Kevin Conde.)

ON THE COVER: This February 1914 photograph captures the old Granger meetinghouse. Whether for Sunday meetings, community activities, dance parties, or holiday celebrations, from 1912–1960 this building was the heart of a large part of what would someday become West Valley City. Looking east, this church was on the southeast corner of 3500 South and 3600 West Streets, facing 3500 South Street—the community's "Main Street." (Courtesy Utah State Historical Society.)

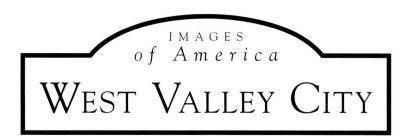

IMAGES
of America

WEST VALLEY CITY

Mayor Mike Winder and the
West Valley City Historical Society

ARCADIA
PUBLISHING

Published by Arcadia Publishing
Charleston, South Carolina

Printed in the United States of America

Library of Congress Control Number: 2012934603

For all general information, please contact Arcadia Publishing:
Telephone 843-853-2070
Fax 843-853-0044
E-mail sales@arcadiapublishing.com
For customer service and orders:
Toll-Free 1-888-313-2665

Visit us on the Internet at www.arcadiapublishing.com

To two of the biggest cheerleaders for West Valley City the community has ever known: Kevin and Margene Conde. Thank you for believing so passionately in our city and me personally!

CONTENTS

ACKNOWLEDGMENTS

West Valley City has had two very good published histories to date. The first, *Under Granger Skies: History of Granger 1849–1963*, was compiled by Rosa Vida Bischoff Black and published by the Granger Stake Relief Society of the Church of Jesus Christ of Latter-day Saints in 1963. The second, *Let's Do It: West Valley City's Official Early History: 1848–1990*, was written by Michael J. Gorrell and published in 1993 by the West Valley City Civic Committee. This book was built on the foundation of these predecessors and drew heavily from them, so my gratitude, first and foremost, goes to Black and Gorrell.

I appreciate the encouragement, proofreading, and photographs shared for this project by members of the West Valley City Historical Society (WVCHS), including Chair D'An Wadsworth, Nicci Wadsworth, Ronald and Barbara Watt, Carolynn Burt, Patricia Rushton, Bill Barton, Jean Pagels, Michael Christensen, and especially Harlan Bangerter. Archivist Ron Watt was particularly helpful.

Ron Fox was critical in helping me gain access to the vast archives of the *Deseret News* (DN) currently housed in the Church of Jesus Christ of Latter-day Saints (LDS) Church History Library, where archivist Bill Slaughter was extremely helpful. The collection of the Utah State Historical Society (USHS) was another great source, and Doug Misner and his team there were also very helpful. For recent images, nobody can beat the thousands of photographs taken by Kevin Conde (KC) for the city. I appreciate Kevin enormously for his historic contribution.

I appreciate Sue Johnson at WalMart and John Brock of Hexcel Corporation, who both arranged for generous financial support to help us share copies of this book. DeAnn Varney has assisted me in gathering information about later images, which was crucial for the captions. Stacia Bannerman, Laura Saylor, and the team at Arcadia Publishing were great to work with and helped me to bring these pages to life as a book.

Thank you to all who have helped in various ways. But most of all, I thank my wife, Karyn, who patiently supports me in doing projects like this and who shares my love for our hometown. Our children, Jessica, Michael, John, and Grace, are the sixth generation of Winders to live on Winder Lane and share our appreciation for West Valley City's past and excitement for a bright future!

—Mayor Mike Winder
December 12, 2011

INTRODUCTION

Mormon prophet Brigham Young declared that someday there would be more inhabitants on the west side of the Jordan River than on the east. He told his friend William Armstrong that "the day will come when there will be large places of manufacture and storage constructed west of the Jordan River, and there will be over three millions of people living there, and Jordan River will practically run through the center of Salt Lake City." Such prophesies would have seemed far-fetched in the mid-19th century, or even the mid-20th century, but at the dawn of the 21st century, half of the valley west of the Jordan River is indeed filling with people, activity, and commerce.

West Valley City is relatively young, though it is Utah's second largest city. Incorporated in 1980, the city does not have the deep civic traditions of older Utah communities like Ogden, Salt Lake City, or Provo. In fact, because the city grew out of farming communities that evolved into suburbs, West Valley City has never had a traditional city center like these older pioneer-founded municipalities with their historic main streets. Rectifying this as the city urbanizes is a major concern of today's city leaders, as they work to not only enhance the tax base, but more importantly, to create a sense of place and civic identity for the community.

The lack of city hall formalities does not mean that there were not good people living in the area for over a hundred years before the incorporation of West Valley City. The first pioneers "over Jordan" in 1848 were Joseph and Susanna Harker's family, and other families soon followed in 1849.

While many of these first families moved farther south to what would become Taylorsville, a wave of new settlers to what was then called "Granger" came beginning in 1866. In the city today, many descendants of these pioneering families endure—bearing names like Rasmussen, Hemenway, Warr, Parks, Holmberg, Bess, Turpin, Todd, Wallace, Barton, Nebeker, Hill, Bawden, and Bangerter.

By the 1870s and 1880s, canals were dug across the west side of the valley, bringing water from the Jordan River. The canals were invaluable for irrigation and allowed settlement farther west. The area of Hunter was settled by families like the Rushtons, Hansens, Bertochs, and Days. By 1900, the farming communities of Hunter and Granger had built churches, schools, and mills. The census showed 354 residents of Hunter and 617 residents of Granger.

A new century brought paved roads (the first being 3500 South Street in 1918), automobiles, more growth, and an interurban rail line that connected people and goods from Magna in the west, to Salt Lake City in the east. Social life still largely revolved around the local Mormon meetinghouse, and the rhythms and routines of life on the farm dictated most families' lifestyles.

After World War II, the residents united in a Granger-Hunter Improvement District. Established in 1950, this organization provided culinary water and modern sewer services, which allowed new subdivisions to become a reality. The residential boom was on.

Farms disappeared or shrunk as suburbia encroached. To fill the needs of the growing community, businesses appeared along major corridors like 3500 South Street and Redwood Road. But growth was somewhat haphazard, and the political leaders of Salt Lake County did not hesitate to place a disproportionate share of the valley's multifamily residential units in the area, for example. Nor did they focus much on the aesthetics of business signage, street infrastructure, or the need for parks and recreation centers.

Area residents began to organize in groups like the Lions Club, Rotary Club, Valley West Chamber of Commerce, and Daughters of the Utah Pioneers. From these civic-minded organizations came the Granger-Hunter Community Council in 1964. After a failed incorporation effort in 1978, West Valley City was officially born on July 1, 1980.

The early years for West Valley City were rough. In fact, new city leaders were faced with a disincorporation vote on the ballot just a week after they were sworn in on July 1. No bank would finance a city that may become defunct within days, so the first city mayor, Hank Price, and city commissioners Renee Mackay and Jerry Wagstaff paid for gas for the police cars out of their own pockets.

Disincorporation failed and the city was here to stay, but the recession of the early 1980s was not kind to the infant municipality. Finances were rough, but prudent management got the city on its feet—even paying cash for a new city hall that was completed in 1990.

More parks were added, new fire stations built, and the boyhood home of the first Kentucky Fried Chicken franchisee Pete Harman was turned into a senior recreation center. A Family Fitness Center was built, as was the Hale Centre Theatre and the E-Center (now Maverik Center) hockey arena. When the Olympics came to Salt Lake in 2002, the primary ice hockey venue was in West Valley City—a source of pride for residents.

Because of its relatively affordable housing, West Valley City was a popular place to settle for new immigrants coming to the Salt Lake Valley—be they from Southeast Asia following the Vietnam War, LDS Pacific Islanders desiring to live near the center of Mormonism, or Hispanic immigrants working in the area. Even as the city's housing stock improved, minority groups felt more comfortable with the relative diversity and continued to settle there. By 2010, West Valley City was Utah's most ethnically diverse city (45 percent minorities).

The Utah Cultural Celebration Center was built in 2003 to help leverage the positive aspects of the diverse community. An English Language Initiative was launched in 2011 to begin to address the challenge of a community in which 31 percent of residents spoke a language other than English at home.

Today, West Valley City has a unique sense of community pride. Perhaps because of the negative stereotypes that people outside the city sometimes perpetuate, residents are extra proud of a city they feel is a good place to live, with great neighbors, a convenient location, excellent city amenities, and nearby city services. Crime is dropping, the shopping mall and oldest high school are being rebuilt, light rail service lends an urban feel, and new jobs are being created at rates much higher than national averages.

Yes, the future of Utah's second largest city is bright. And the city has emerged as more than just a farming area and more than just a bedroom community of Salt Lake City. West Valley City is solidifying its own identity and sense of place and is a success story rooted in the deep legacy celebrated in this history.

One

A New Home
"Over Jordan"
1848–1899

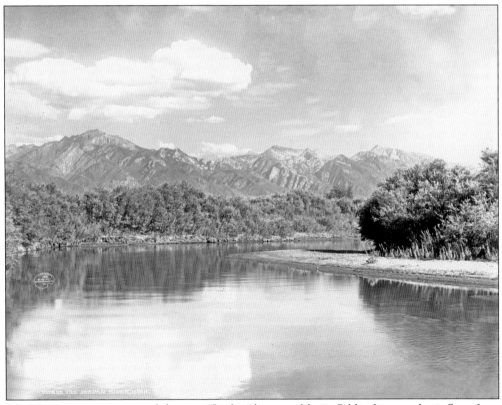

The Mormon pioneers named the river "Jordan" because, like its Biblical namesake, it flows from a freshwater lake into the saltiest lake in the hemisphere. Bisecting the valley of the Great Salt Lake, the land west of the Jordan River was being eyed only a year after the Mormon pioneers first entered the valley in 1847. This is a c. 1900 photograph of the River Jordan. (Photograph by William Henry Jackson; courtesy Library of Congress.)

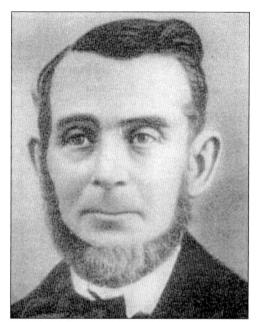 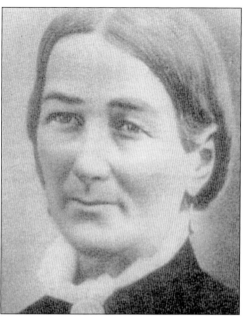

Joseph and Susanna Smeath Harker were Mormon converts from England who crossed the plains to Utah, arriving in 1847. In the fall of 1848, they became the first pioneers "over Jordan," crossing near today's 3300 South Street to procure grass for their animals. Joseph sold the log cabin he had built in exchange for two oxen, and the Harkers moved south to Taylorsville the following year. (WVCHS.)

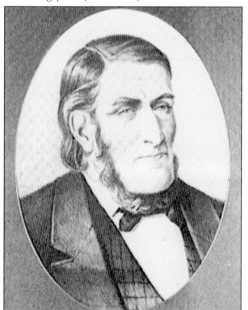 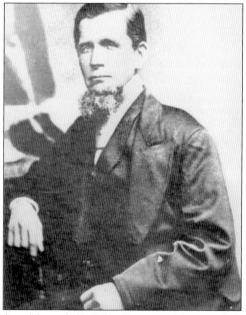

On January 9, 1849, the families of Thomas Mackay (above left), John Bennion (above right), Samuel Bennion, Thomas Tarbet, William Farrer, William Blackhurst, and John Robinson crossed the Jordan River on ice and joined the Harkers on the west bank. That winter, they lived in dugouts alongside the river. In the spring, they moved a mile south to plant crops and enjoy a small harvest. (WVCHS.)

More families came west and began settling beyond the riverbeds and onto the "flats," where land was more fertile. Canals dug in the 1870s and 1880s brought water to the area, which Salt Lake County judge Elias Smith named "Granger" because of its productive farmland. This photograph shows settlers haying in Granger around 1900. (Photograph by William Henry Jackson; courtesy Library of Congress.)

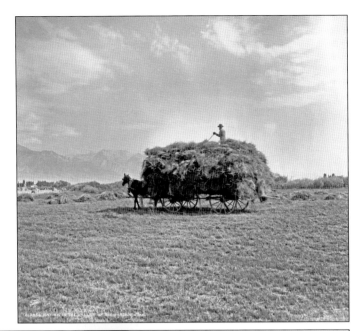

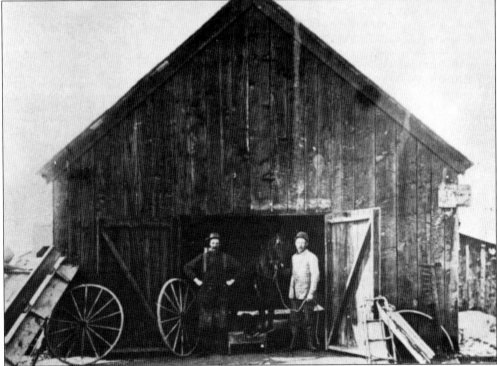

Among the early businesses was a blacksmith shop and small store, built in 1883 at 3525 South 3200 West by Joseph Watson Fairbourne. Fairbourne appears on the left of this photograph, with neighbor Frederick Nielsen on the right. Here, produce was weighed and church tithes levied before the farmers proceeded to Murray or Salt Lake City to sell their goods. The Fairbourne weigh station was the focal point of the farming community and included the area's first post office. (WVCHS.)

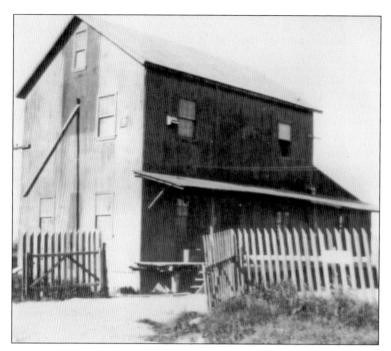

Swiss immigrants Frederick and Alice Bangerter built a flourmill at 3650 South 3600 West Street. In 1892, they expanded their small coffee mill into a wheat grinder using a small gasoline engine, and in 1902, they upgraded to a larger engine and grinder. Farmers would come from miles around to grind wheat for pigs, roll grain for horses, and make flour for baked goods. (WVCHS.)

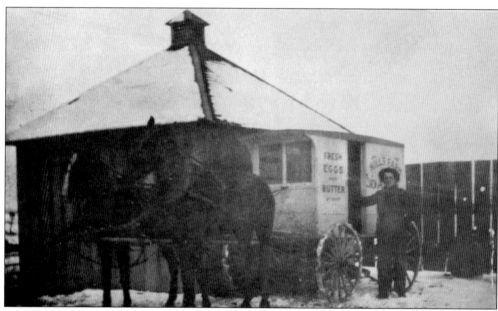

Edgar "Ted" Hill made the rounds in early Granger, selling eggs, butter, and other dairy products from his Hills Farm Dairy. Ted grew up in Granger in a brick home at 2653 West 3500 South Street. For 16 years, he was the activity counselor for the young men and young women in the area, organizing dances and other activities. (WVCHS.)

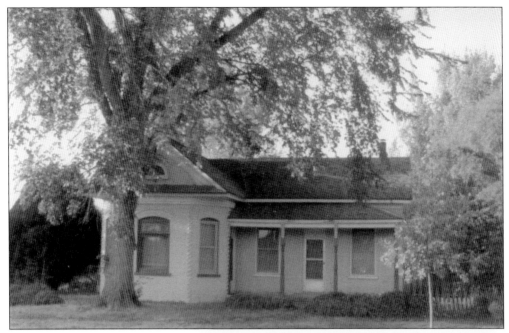

The William Mackay home was built in the 1880s at 1988 West 4100 South Street. It is one of the oldest homes still standing in the city. After their wedding in 1882, Mackay and his bride, Margaret Ellen Part, built a log home on this site. After a fire destroyed the house, Mackay built a two-room brick house and later added three more rooms. They reared 10 children here. (WVCHS.)

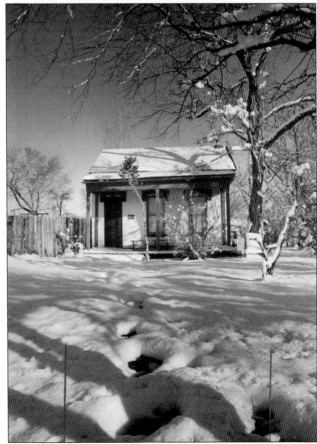

The William McLachlan farmhouse was built in 1884 at 4499 South 3200 West Street. It was added to the National Register of Historic Places in 1980. Other pioneer homes along 3200 West Street include the homes of Josiah Davis Wallace, William Henry Derr, Marcus Bennion, Archie Bennion, Lachonius Luther Hemenway, and Joseph Fairbourne. (DN.)

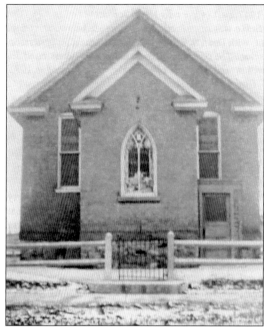

As canals supplying reliable water were dug in the 1870s, farmers began settling west of Granger. The area was named for the LDS presiding bishop Edward Hunter, and the Mormons built this adobe chapel there in 1885. Scandinavian converts in Hunter met in the home of Fred Hansen from 1879 to 1884, when their services were merged with their English-speaking neighbors. The Hunter Ward was formally organized in 1888. (WVCHS.)

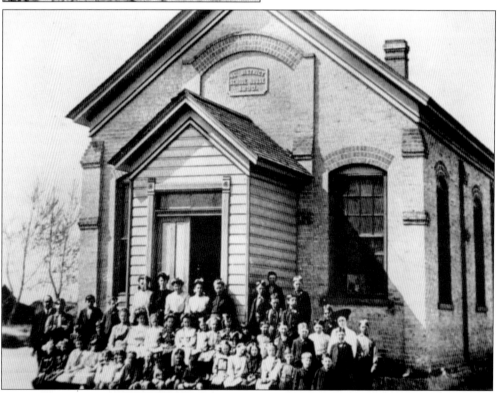

The first brick schoolhouse in the area was the 46th District School, built in 1890 at 2200 West and 3500 South Streets. In September 1906, it was renamed the Granger School, and in May 1908, it was renamed the East Granger School. Eventually, it was called the Dewey School. Principals included C.W. Aldrich, Lorilla Horne, Ethelyn Bennion, and Alice Mackay. (WVCHS.)

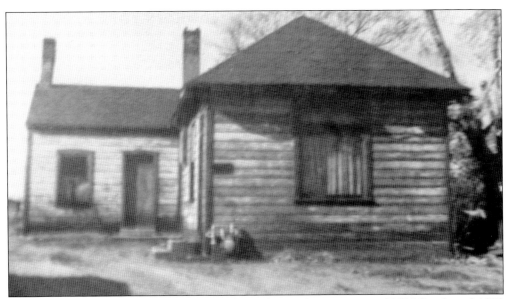

In 1883, a one-room meetinghouse was built on the northwest corner of 3500 South and 4000 West Streets. The Granger Ward, a Mormon congregation, was organized here on February 24, 1884. It was the community-gathering place where school was taught and dances held. An extension of the building was added in 1885. The Granger Ward met here until its new chapel was completed in 1896. (WVCHS.)

The first bishop of the Granger Ward, Daniel McRae, made it a priority to build a proper meetinghouse. The 145 members raised $50 to buy an acre from Isaac Hunter on the southeast corner of 3200 West and 3500 South Streets. They spent the next 11 years building a brick, adobe-lined chapel. Completed in 1896, it had a commodious basement recreation hall, which was the social center in Granger at the turn of the century. (WVCHS.)

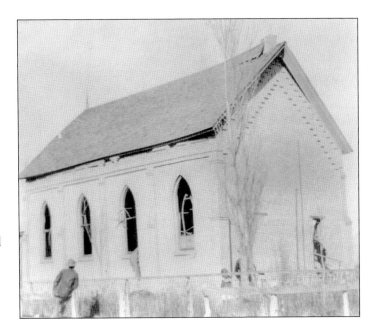

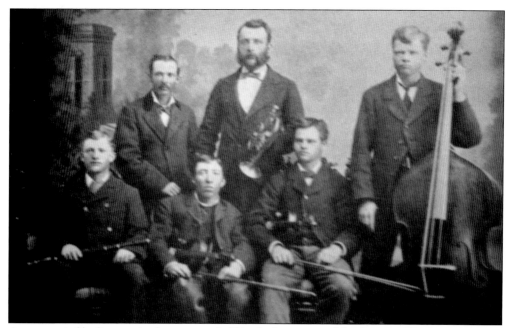

Accompanied by live music, dances were held in the basement of the Granger Ward at the turn of the century. These old-time Granger band members are, from left to right (first row) unidentified, Nathaniel Bawden, and John Sutherland; (second row) Henry L. Bawden, William V. Morris, and leader Joseph Sutherland. The waltz, two-step, polka, and quadrille were popular dances to tunes like "Let Me Call You Sweetheart" and "Good Night Ladies." (WVCHS.)

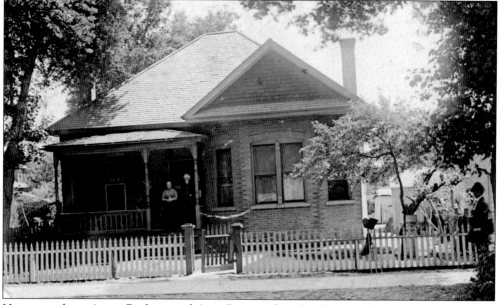

Hunter residents Annie Rushton and Arzie Day stand on the front porch while the letter carrier approaches. This home is on the south side of 4100 South Street facing north at 5400 West Street. By 1900, the US Census counted 354 residents in Hunter and 617 residents in Granger. Together, these 971 souls represented just 1.3 percent of Salt Lake County's population of 77,725. (Courtesy Patricia Rushton.)

Two

GROWING WEST IN A NEW CENTURY
1900–1945

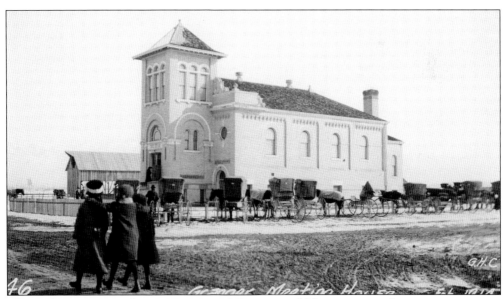

The 20th century saw the communities of Granger and Hunter mature from just a scattering of farms west of the Jordan River into real, cohesive communities, with schools, churches, and traditions. Chesterfield would also take shape in the early 20th century, and landmarks such as the new Granger Ward meetinghouse shown here in February 1914 would help create a sense of place. (USHS.)

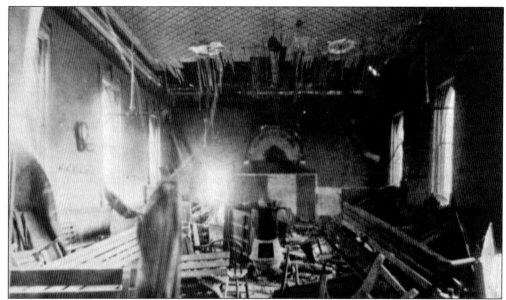

At 8:00 p.m. on March 7, 1905, a gas heater exploded during a dance at the Granger Ward building. The walls collapsed, killing 21-year-old organist Nellie Mackay. This photograph of the inside of the building shows the extensive damage from the tragedy, which made the building unusable. The building was torn down, and within three weeks, ground was broken for a new church on the same site. (WVCHS.)

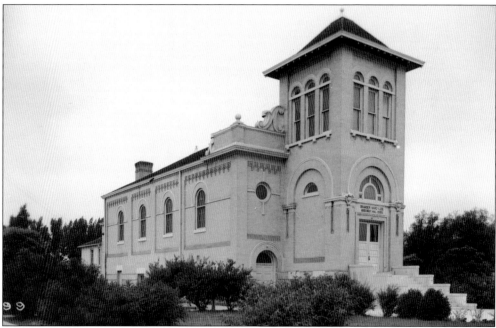

After the tragic explosion at the Granger Ward in 1905, the community rallied to replace the damaged building with a grand meetinghouse. This two-story, yellow-brick assembly hall was a landmark on the southeast corner of 3200 West and 3500 South Streets until it was torn down in 1960. Noted Utah photographer Hal Rumel took this photograph of the landmark in the 1950s. (USHS.)

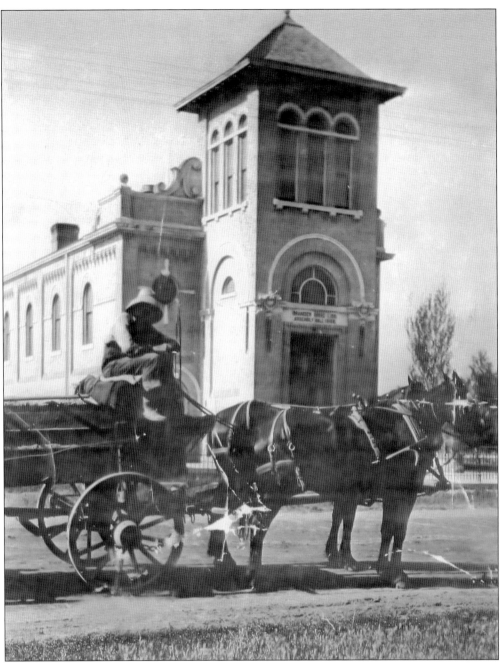

Pres. Joseph F. Merrill dedicated the Granger Ward chapel on February 22, 1912. In 1918, the chapel had the honor of being the first building in the area with electric lights. The ward boundaries extended from the Jordan River on the east to 4800 West Street on the west. LDS church president Thomas S. Monson recalled attending many meetings in the Granger Ward building as a boy, when he would come out to Granger to stay on his grandfather Thomas Condie's farm. He noted that large curtains were used to divide up the spacious room into various Sunday school classes. Brick mason Manassah Smith did such a good job that demolition of the chapel in 1960 was especially difficult. (WVCHS.)

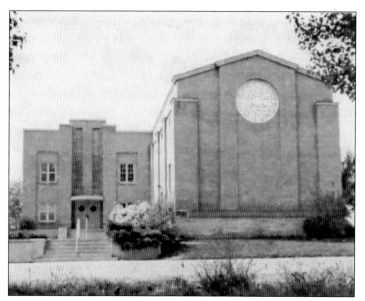

The old Hunter Ward building on 3500 South and 6000 West Streets was the religious center for the Mormons in Hunter. It was also the center of numerous community activities, dances, ball games, and dinners. The Hunter Ward had 137 members in 1888. Membership continued to grow, necessitating additions to the original structure in the decades ahead. (Courtesy Joyce Williams.)

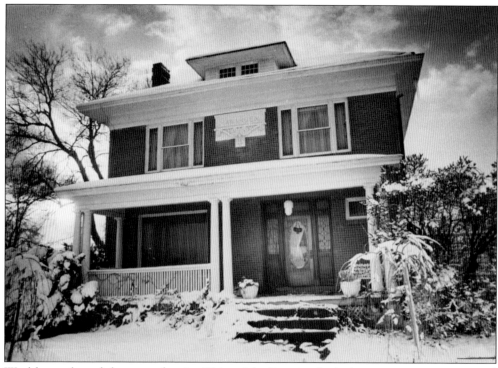

Wealthy cattle and sheep rancher Ira Wainwright Bennion built the impressive two-story, red brick home at 4396 South 3200 West Street in 1906. He named it "Hawarden" after his father's boyhood hometown in Wales, and 8 of his 15 children were born in the house. Bennion died in 1927. The home was put on the National Register of Historic Places in 1980. (DN.)

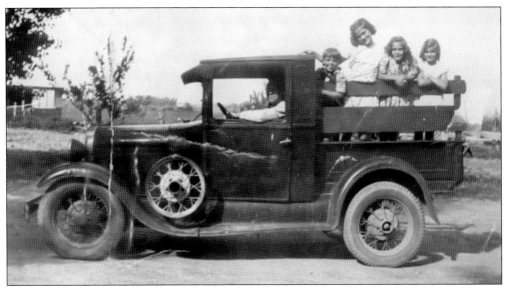

Pictured from left to right, Will Bangerter hauls children Norm, Gleneth, Marian, and Naomi Bangerter on 3200 West Street in 1939. William served as bishop of the LDS Granger Ward from 1920 to 1933. As bishop, he helped move the old tithing barn, landscaped and improved the grounds of the Granger Ward, and encouraged Ruth and Nathan Hale to write an original play, since the ward budget could not afford royalties. (WVCHS.)

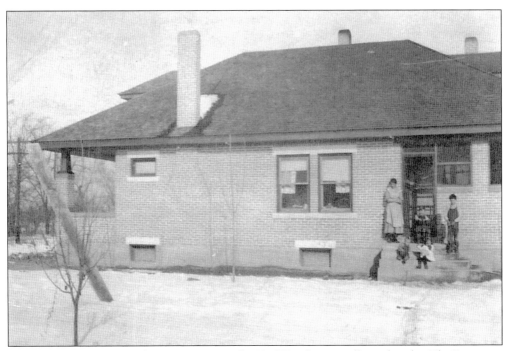

The William H. Bangerter home on 3837 South 3200 West Streets still stands today. The Bangerter family first came to Granger in 1891, and William was a second-generation resident. His children and grandchildren would also live in the community. This is how the Bangerter home appeared in December 1920. (WVCHS.)

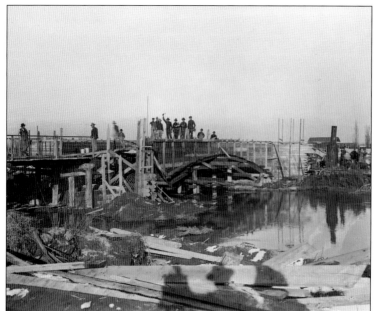

In pioneer times, seasonal crossings over the ice were common as there were very few bridges over the Jordan River. As the settlements over Jordan grew, more sophisticated bridges were required. In 1905, a substantial bridge was built over the Jordan River at 3300 South Street, connecting what was essentially the main street of Hunter and Granger with the rest of the Salt Lake Valley. (USHS.)

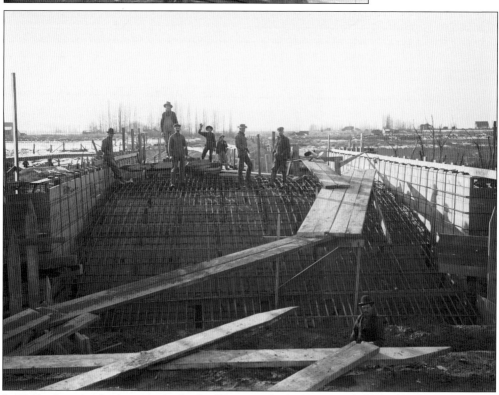

In 1905, when this bridge over the Jordan River was built, 3300 South Street was known as 1400 South Street. Street numbers were modernized by the Salt Lake City Commission on May 12, 1916, and 12th South Street became 2100 South Street, 13th South Street became 2700 South Street, 14th South Street became 3300 South Street, 15th South Street became 3900 South Street, 16th South Street became 4500 South Street, and so forth. (USHS.)

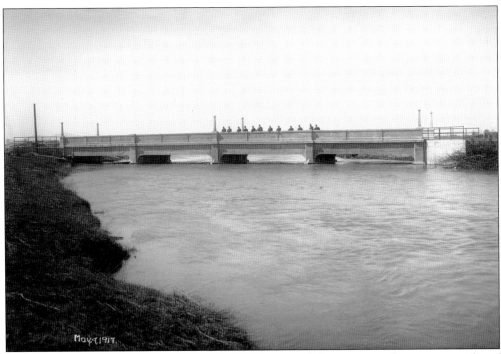

The construction of a bridge over the Jordan River at 2100 South Street was another engineering feat of the era. This photograph was taken as the bridge neared completion on May 9, 1917. (USHS.)

Ethel Shafer Holmberg and her sons Wayne and Chester wait for a train at the station at 1950 West 3500 South Street. On October 10, 1917, the 9.7-mile Magna branch of the Salt Lake and Utah Interurban Railway opened for service with eight daily trains, connecting west side residents with the main line that ran from Salt Lake to Payson. The main line was called the Orem Line, after developer A.J. Orem. By the late 1920s, the main line supported 18 trains a day, carrying passengers, mail, and freight, as well as students to and from Cyprus High School in Magna. The trains were abandoned for financial reasons, and the last run was on March 1, 1946. (WVCHS.)

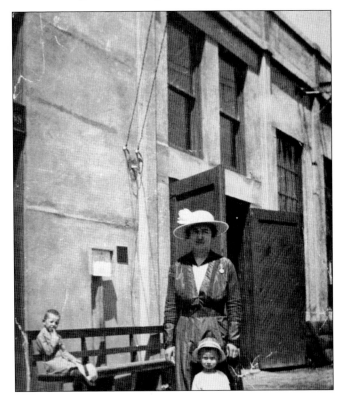

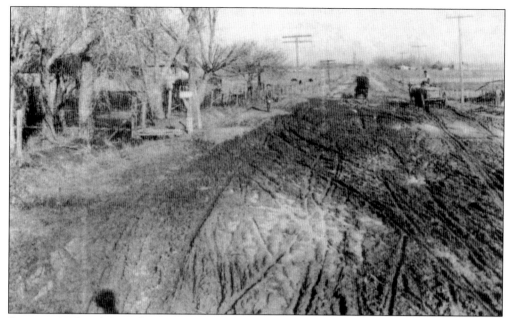

Between 1915 and 1918, drains were dug to eliminate swampy sections of 3500 South Street. A concrete surface was poured when the drains were complete, and 3500 South Street (for years, dusty in the summer and muddy in the spring) became the first paved street on the west side and a part of the coast-to-coast Lincoln Highway. Snowplows were in use by 1925. This 1916 photograph of 3500 South Street looking east was taken from 3200 West Street. (WVCHS.)

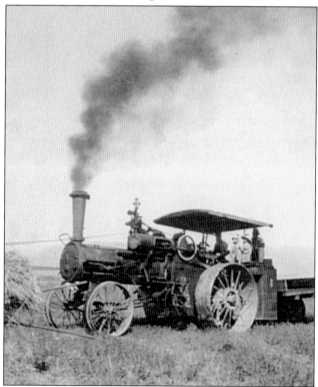

One of the major chores on the farm was threshing—the separation of the grain from the stalks and the husks. The owners of this steam thresher loaned it to farmers for 14 bushels of each 100 threshed. This photograph shows the last visit of the steam thresher to the farms of Granger and Hunter in 1937. (WVCHS.)

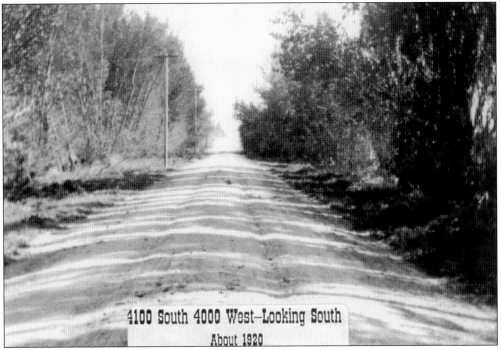

4100 South 4000 West—Looking South
About 1920

This photograph shows 4000 West Street when it was still a dirt road. In the 1920s, Ned and Rich Winder laid down on the sun-warmed pavement of 4100 South Street on cool spring days. Every 30 minutes or so the boys would have to get out of the road when an automobile would come through. (WVCHS.)

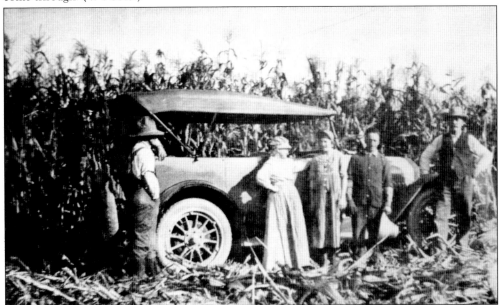

Seen here on their Granger farm are, from left to right, Grover Hill, mother Betsy Hill, Vinnie Hill, William D. Hill, and father A.J. Hill. Alexander Joseph Hill (1860–1926) married Betsy Ann Bawden in 1884, and they lived in Granger for the rest of their lives. He was superintendent of the North Jordan Canal, constable of Granger, and, later, justice of the peace. (WVCHS.)

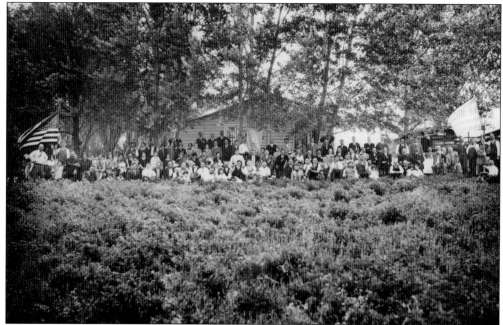

This early 1920s image shows Greek residents from Garfield picnicking on the Jordan River shore in Chesterfield. Although encouraged by the Kimball and Richards Company, the original settlement of Chesterfield in 1914 did not last. It was the homes built during the 1930s that gave Chesterfield its first permanent residents. (USHS.)

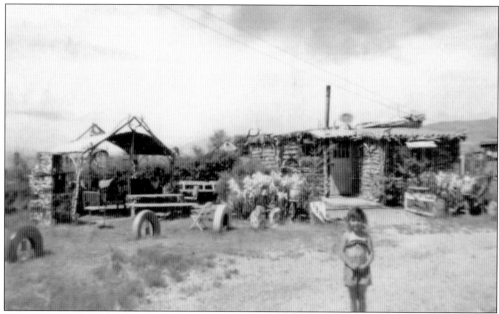

During the Great Depression, 110 families built houses in the Chesterfield area near 2100 South Street and the Jordan River with the help of the county welfare department. The conditions of these Chesterfield homes were extremely poor. Most dwellings consisted of only two rooms and lacked both central heat and bathtubs. This is one of the earliest homes built in Chesterfield at 1364 West Parkway Boulevard, as it appeared in the 1960s. (WVCHS.)

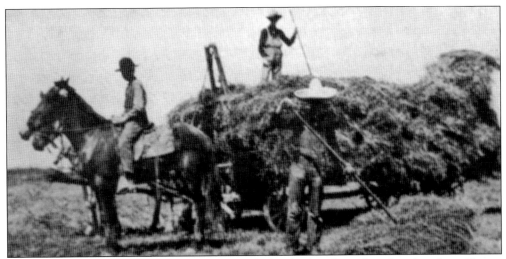

Charles John Lambert is on the horse in front of the hay load, with son Joseph and nephews George H. Lambert and George L. Woodbury assisting in loading the hay. At that time, loading piles of alfalfa onto a hay wagon was a ritual that occurred every June, July, and September. (WVCHS.)

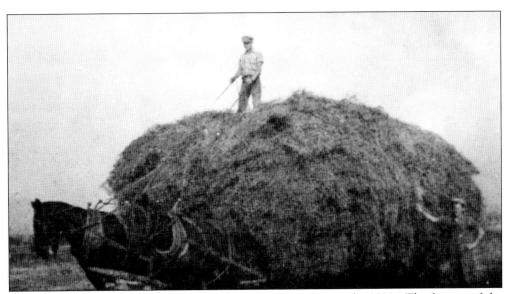

Shown here, Rulon and Newell Mackay take in a load of hay in the 1930s. The farmers of the area would leave at 6 a.m., stopping at the Fairbourne scales at 3200 West and 3500 South Streets to weigh the load and continuing into town to sell the hay. It was mostly the city cows that got this choice hay. (WVCHS.)

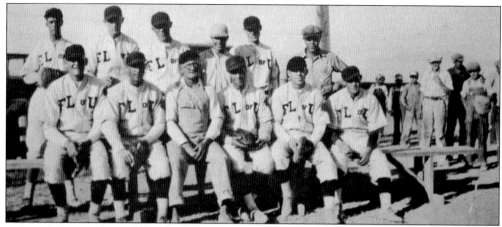

Granger's first baseball team, from left to right, included (first row) William "Bill" Lehman, Clem Bolton, coach Edgar "Ted" Hill, Edward "Ted" Bolton, Smith Bawden, and Bill Warr; (second row) Wayne Irving, Frank Bolton, Severn Smith, Conrad Gerber, Ren Butcher, and Ike Gerber. They belonged to the Farm Bureau League and traveled all over the county making quite a name for Granger with their successes. (WVCHS.)

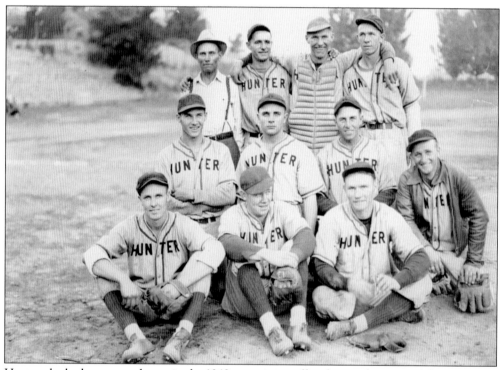

Hunter also had a very good team in the 1940s, consisting of brothers and cousins of the prominent Rushton family. This photograph of the team, taken at Hunter Park (3600 South and 6000 West Streets), shows their coach Albert Rushton (upper left), Laurence Rushton (in the center), Lewis Rushton (far right with mitt), and Sylvester "Sly" Rushton (bottom right), among other family members. (Courtesy Elva Rushton.)

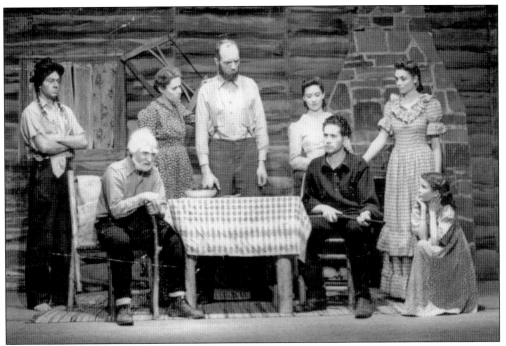

Plays were a popular activity of the church. In 1937, Ruth and Nathan Hale were asked to write a play for the Granger Ward. *It Shall Keep Thee* starred the following actors, from left to right: (first row) Liston Parr, Nathan Hale, and Maurine Inkley; (second row) Sam Bangerter, Ruth Neilsen, Glenn Todd, Phyllis Park, and LaRue Latimer. The Hales would go on to operate theaters in California and Utah. (WVCHS.)

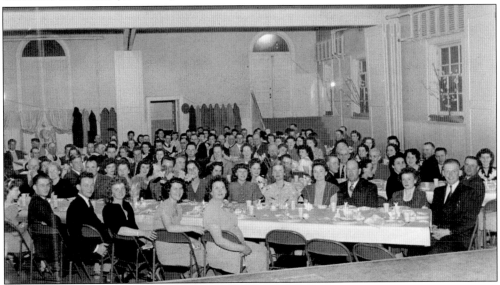

The spacious basement of the Granger Ward building held numerous social activities in the community—like this April Fool's Day dinner in 1947. Dances were usually held each Friday evening, when the hall would be packed with young and old. Everybody danced. Cold orange cider and refreshments were served in a little room at the north end of the hall, known as the "cider room." (WVCHS.)

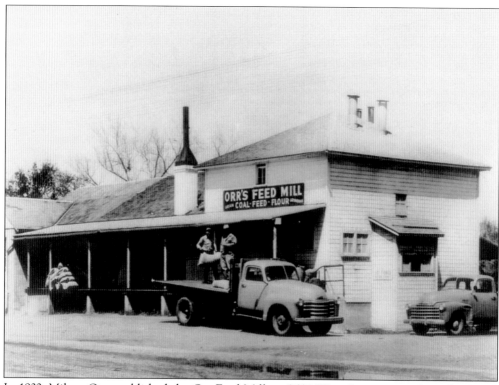

In 1932, Milton Orr established the Orr Feed Mill on 3600 West Street across from the future Granger High School. Here, Orr engaged in milling, buying, and processing grain for seed, feed, and dairy mix. In 1940, he moved the business to the northeast corner of 3600 West and 3500 South Streets. His son Max Orr helped carry on the business, which grew to include feed, seed, coal, hay, and fertilizers. They reported serving customers from as far away as Tremonton and Ibapah (on the Nevada border). (Both, WVCHS.)

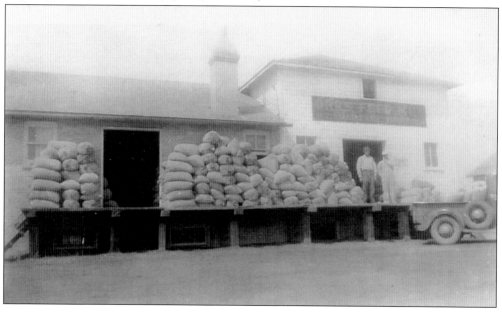

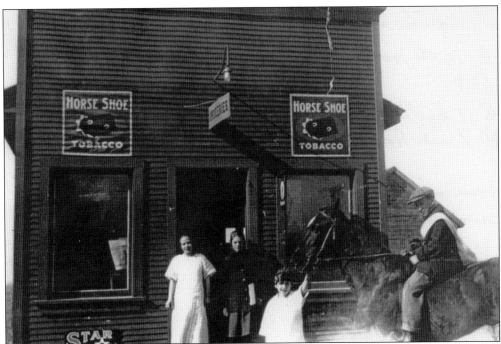

The Cannon Store, located at the northeast corner of 4000 West and 3500 South Streets, upgraded its storefront in the 1920s. The store is seen in these photographs both before and after renovations. As the only grocery store for miles in its day, the small store included dry goods, housedresses, hardware, meats brought in by Wirthlin Meats, and penny candy, which was popular with the children of the nearby Monroe School. Most items were located behind the counter, and customers can remember how Peggy Cannon would hum and sing as she helped gather items on their lists. At noon, Cannon would also make hamburgers that she sold for 5¢. The store closed when she retired in 1956. (Both, WVCHS.)

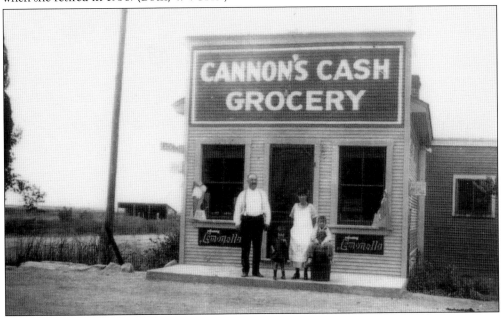

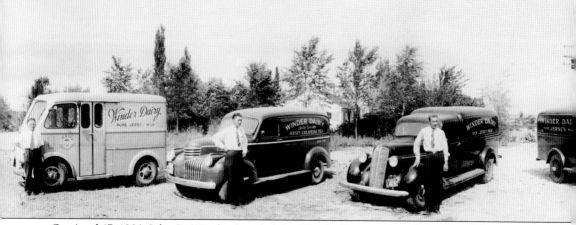

On April 17, 1880, John R. Winder founded the Winder Dairy and made his first deliveries. The dairy was originally headquartered at 2700 South and 400 East Streets in what is now South Salt Lake. Due to a boll weevil infestation on the east side of the valley, the family began buying farmland around 4400 West and 4100 South Streets beginning in 1910. In 1919, grandson J.R. "Jack" Winder started the J.R. Winder Dairy at 2470 West 3500 South Street, delivering dairy products in areas not covered by the original business. In the meantime, Jack Winder's brothers George and Ed Winder started the Winder Brothers Dairy at 4400 West and 4100 South Streets,

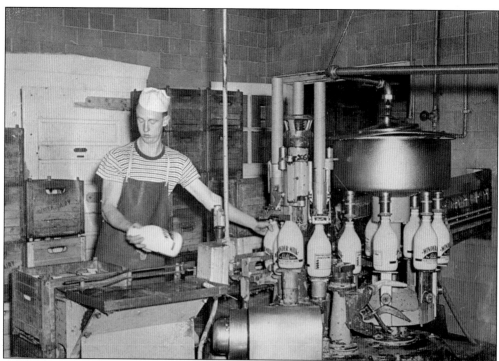

Milk is being bottled at the Winder Dairy plant in the 1940s. The long-necked bottles were appealing for the unhomogenized milk because customers liked to see the cream float up to the top of the bottles. Winder Dairy has employed thousands of area residents through its century-plus history. (Courtesy Winder Farms.)

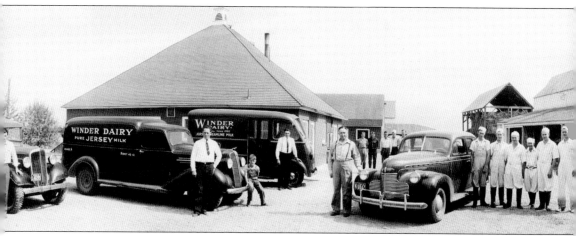

delivering products to the Magna-Garfield areas to the west. On July 4, 1931, all three dairies combined to their present location on 4400 West Street. This 1941 panorama shows general manager George Winder by his car, with nephews Rich and Ned Winder in the center of the group behind him. Another nephew David "Jers" Winder sits on the bumper of the milk truck. He would grow up to be a federal judge and to swear in the very first West Valley City mayor and commission. (Courtesy Winder Farms.)

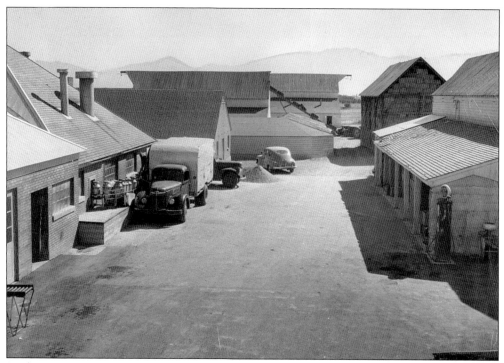

Looking east across the dairy yard in the 1940s, the milk plant is on the left, and a truck is seen unloading milk cans. This building was used as a bakery from 1958 to 2007. The milking parlor is adjacent to the east and was turned into the Winder Country Store in 1983. (Courtesy Winder Farms.)

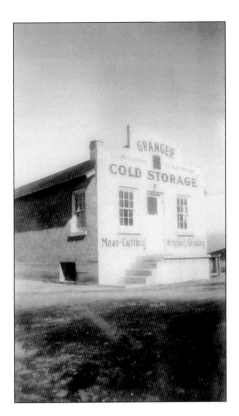

In 1939, Al Warr opened Granger Cold Storage at 3550 West 3500 South Street with a capacity of 185 lockers. In 1948, the capacity of the plant expanded to 550 lockers and was renamed the Warr Locker Plant. Back in the early days of electric refrigeration, owning a freezer was luxury; so, people would rent a frozen locker here. (WVCHS.)

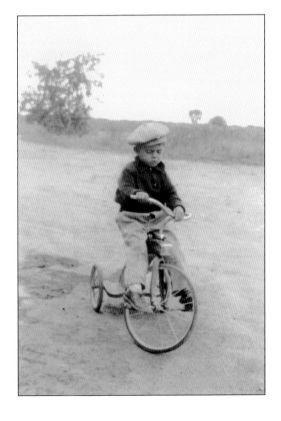

Utah's 13th governor, Norm Bangerter, was born in Granger on January 4, 1933, and grew up on 3200 West Street. Here, he is as a young boy riding his tricycle in the 1930s. Bangerter would later represent the area in the Utah House of Representatives from 1975 to 1985 and was governor of the state from 1985 to 1993. (WVCHS.)

The 59th District School was completed in 1903 at 4000 West and 3500 South Streets. Also known as the West Granger School, it was renamed after a major extension in 1909 to honor America's fifth president, James Monroe. Originally, the school had one principal and only one teacher. In 1914, Monroe was one of the first schools in the state to add a junior-high program for older students. (WVCHS.)

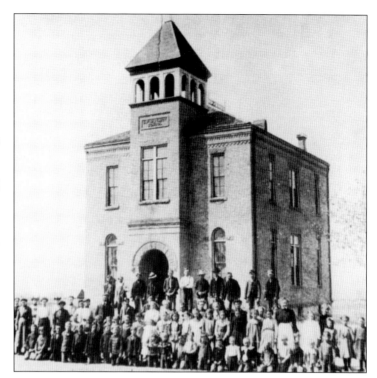

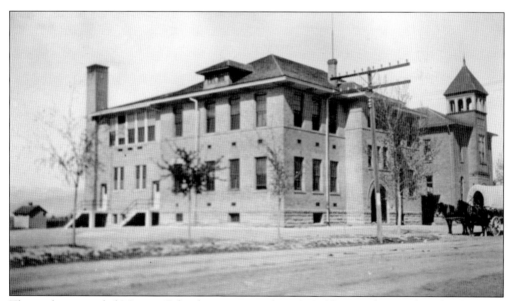

This is the expanded Monroe School as it appeared in 1916. Also seen here is the school wagon, a forerunner of the school bus. This wagon would travel the old farm roads, picking up students each morning and later taking them home. Drivers would have big rocks or bricks (that their wives had heated) nestled in the straw to keep the children's feet warm. (Photograph by Newell Beeman; courtesy USHS.)

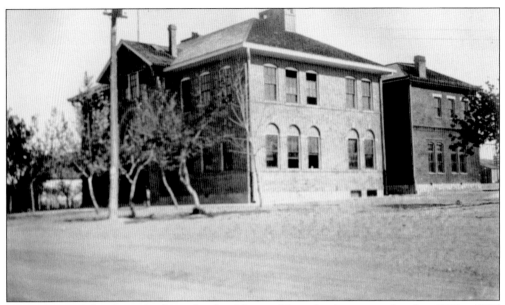

The Whittier School was the first school in Hunter. The school was completed in 1905 at 5975 West 3500 South Street. Originally called the 50th District School, it was renamed the Hunter School in September 1906, and then the Whittier School in May 1908. A 1909 addition to the school is seen in this 1916 photograph. Other additions occurred in 1939 and 1955. (Photograph by Newell Beeman; courtesy USHS.)

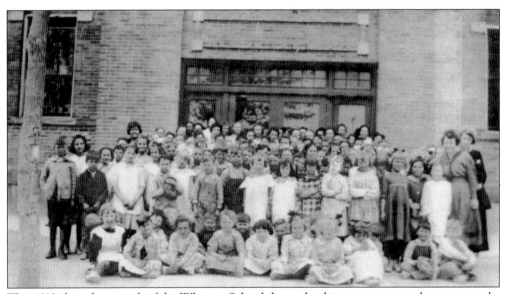

This 1919 class photograph of the Whittier School shows the diverse age groups that were taught together. Carrie Larsen was the principal at the time, serving from 1918 to 1920. In 1923, a 24-year-old educator Harold B. Lee was named principal and a teacher at the school. Lee taught at Whittier until 1925 and later became president of the LDS church. (WVCHS.)

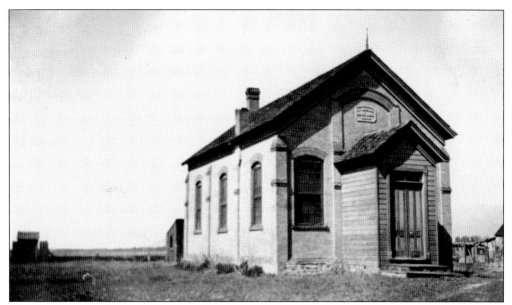

The Dewey School at 2200 West 3500 South Street was abandoned once the Monroe School opened in 1908. The school had truancy issues with the older boys, who would often wander off to Decker Lake. The building was vacant when Newell Beeman took this photograph in 1916. On August 13, 1917, the property was sold to John Wendel for $359. (USHS.)

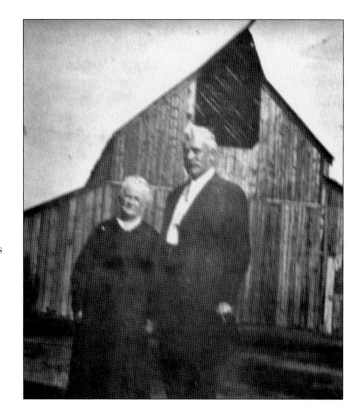

This 1920s photograph shows Alexander Joseph Hill and Betsy Ann Bawden Hill in front of their old barn—a Granger landmark torn down in 1962 to make way for a shopping center. The Hill farmstead was next door to Jacob Hunter's at 2700 West and 3500 South Streets. (WVCHS.)

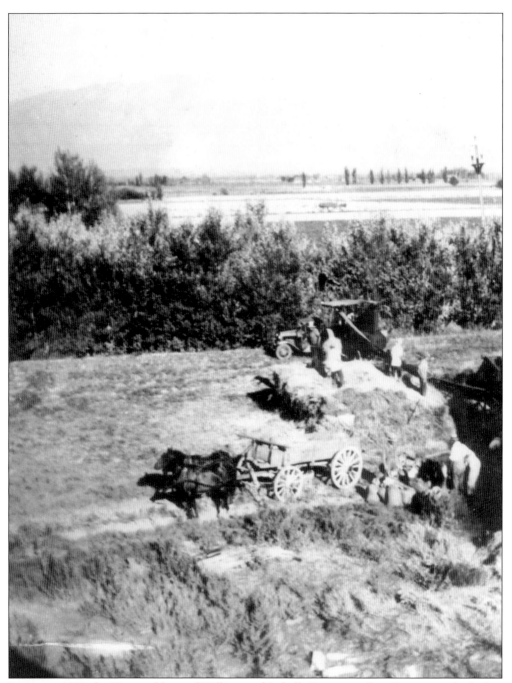

In August 1937, the 17-year-old son of William and Isabelle Bangerter, Sam Bangerter, climbed to the top of the old Jacob Hunter barn to take this photograph of a typical Granger threshing scene. The tall Hunter barn from which the photograph was taken was a landmark for miles around. In the east, Mount Olympus and the Wasatch Mountains are visible. On the upper right of the photograph, a power pole carries many wires along 2700 West Street, which is sometimes called "Pole Line Road." The field in the foreground is the site of the future West Valley City Hall, and the field beyond the trees is where Valley Fair Mall and Interstate 215 sit today. (WVCHS.)

Three

POSTWAR BOOM

1946–1975

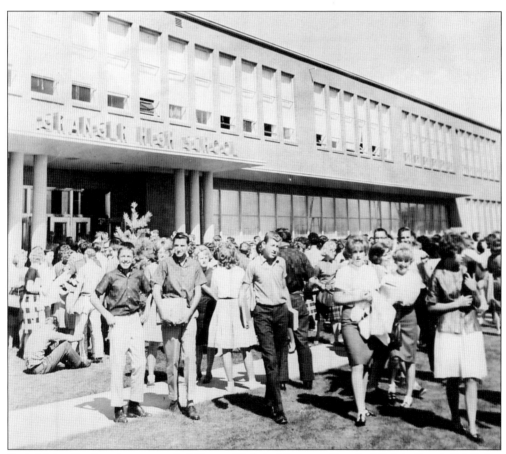

Early high school students attended Cyprus High in Magna or Granite High in South Salt Lake. In the fall of 1958, the first 900 students entered the new Granger High School at 3600 South 3600 West Street. This photograph shows students being evacuated from the new school after a 5.2-magnitude earthquake in Magna shook the area at 9:04 a.m. on September 5, 1962. (DN.)

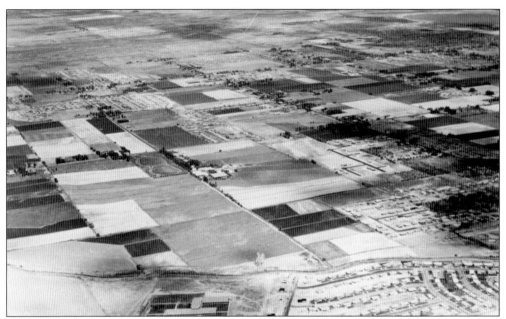

This 1954 aerial photograph shows the neighborhoods to the northeast that began to sprout up in Granger after World War II. The Utah and Salt Lake Canal flows in the foreground, with 4400 West Street running north from the canal through Winder Dairy. A figure-eight road of the community's first cemetery is seen towards the center left of the photograph. Valley View Memorial Park had its first interment on October 25, 1954. (DN.)

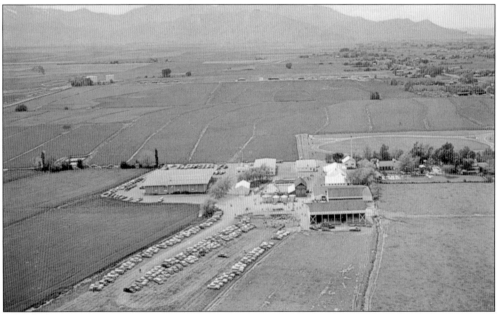

This 1960 aerial photograph shows Winder Dairy in the foreground. Cars are parked outside the dairy for a customer appreciation day. The dairy and adjacent cemetery are located on 4400 West Street. A few homes dot the street, and the new water tanks of the Granger-Hunter Improvement District are in view. In the upper-right corner, a more-developed 4100 South Street runs west to Magna and the Oquirrh Mountains. (Courtesy Winder Farms.)

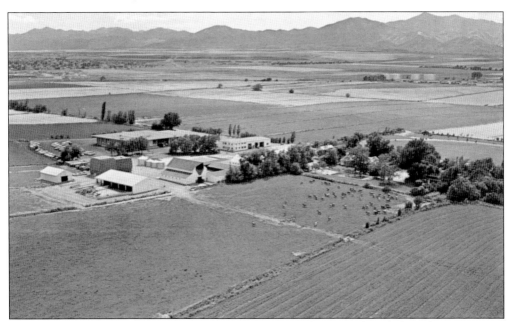

This 1964 aerial photograph shows Winder Dairy in the foreground, including the cows out to pasture. Developed during World War II, the community of Kearns is seen in the upper-left corner. The water tanks off 4800 West Street are in the upper right of the photograph. The beautiful Oquirrh Mountains are visible in the background, to the southwest. (Courtesy Winder Farms.)

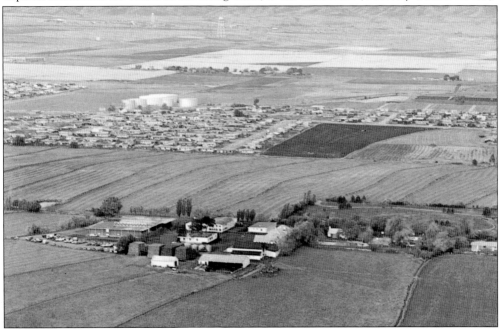

This 1971 aerial photograph shows Winder Dairy and the Valley View Memorial Park. In the upper left corner, full subdivisions have appeared around 4800 West Street and south of 4700 South Street. More homes are also visible along 5600 West Street, and in the distance, the new red-and-white-checkered water tower rises at 6400 West and 4800 South Streets. (Courtesy Winder Farms.)

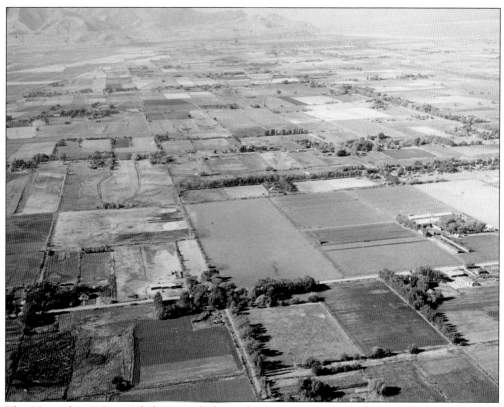

This November 1953 aerial photograph shows the farms in Hunter before any subdivisions came to the area. Looking toward the west, the Oquirrh Mountains are in the distance, with dry farms in the upper left and the Great Salt Lake in the upper right. (DN.)

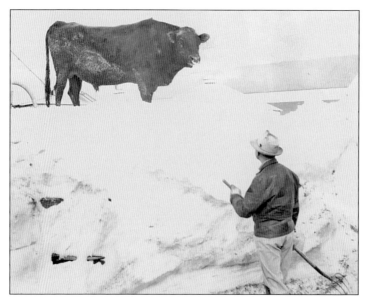

The winter of 1948–1949 was the coldest and snowiest in Utah's recorded history. It hit Granger and Hunter hard. George Winder, manager at Winder Dairy, surveys a snowdrift that was so high cattle were getting stuck. One night, a blizzard stranded all of the milkmen downtown. They had to stay at a hotel and borrow milk from another dairy to service the next day's routes. (Courtesy Winder Farms.)

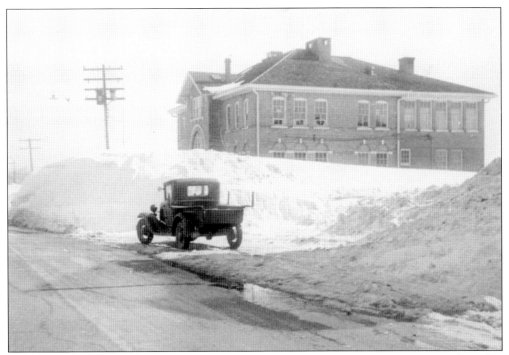

The Whittier School at 5975 West 3500 South Street was one of many schools across the valley that was not only snowed in during January and February of 1949, but was unable to be heated because gas supplies could not meet demand. Electricity was cut off at times because coal companies could not get their coal to Utah Power and Light for its generators. (Courtesy Joyce Williams.)

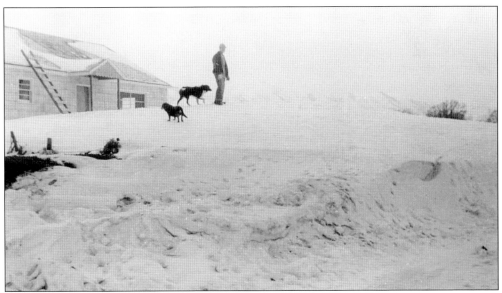

John "Jack" Williams stands atop the snow in front of his house at 5200 West 4100 South Street. The road was so buried that they gave up trying to plow it. Residents of Hunter would have to park on 5600 West Street and hike to their homes. Cold Arctic air chilled the Salt Lake Valley to 25 degrees below zero and kept the snow around for weeks. (Courtesy Joyce Williams.)

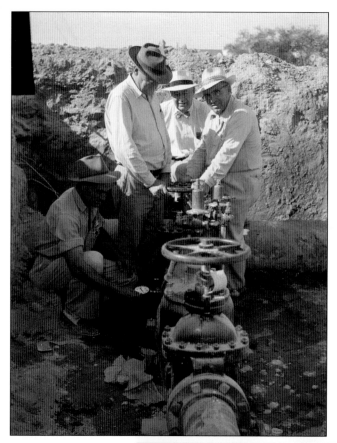

Growth was stifled in the area as long as residents had to rely on well water for drinking and septic tanks for waste. The Granger-Hunter Improvement District was created by the Salt Lake County Commission on January 13, 1950, and the community set out to build a modern water and sewer system. Here, Granger-Hunter officials turn on the first pipes on August 22, 1952. (USHS.)

A January 1953 public vote passed 684 to 37 to authorize $260,000 in bonds to expand the culinary water system. Here, the first trenches are being dug for a 31-mile expansion of the Granger-Hunter Improvement District's pipeline. Pictured here are, from left to right, consulting engineer David I. Gardner, trustee Estel L. Wright, district supervisor Clinton M. Black, and chair of the board of trustees L. O. Larson. (WVCHS.)

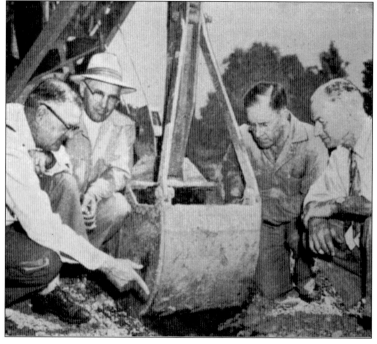

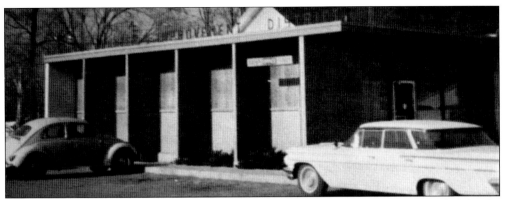

The Granger-Hunter Improvement District provided the critical infrastructure needed for the thousands of homes that would be built in the decades ahead. At the end of 1953, there were 350 homes with water connections, and the district began adding about 250 connections per month. By 1963, there were 5,000 connections. Its original headquarters was located in an office on 3146 West 3500 South Street. (WVCHS.)

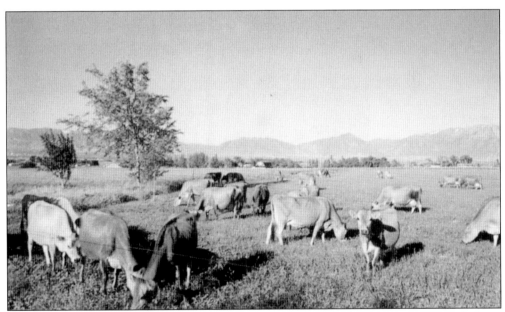

Looking east from Winder Dairy at about 4400 West and 4200 South, this 1959 photograph shows a herd of Jersey cows in the foreground. The empty fields beyond are the future sites of Deno Drive and Falcon Street neighborhoods. The Wasatch Range is in the background, with Mount Olympus on the far right. The dairy herd was removed from Granger in 1973 as the suburbs grew. (Courtesy Winder Farms.)

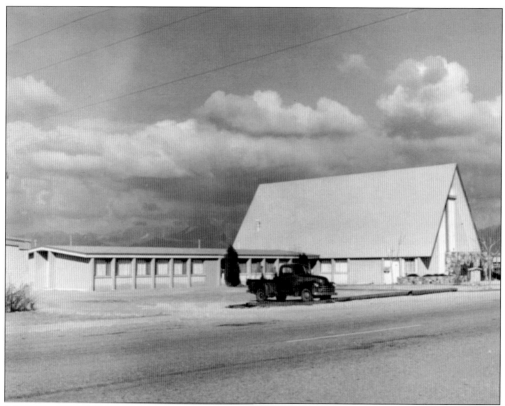

The Granger Christian Community Church was the first Protestant church west of the Jordan River. The church held its first service on September 8, 1957, in a home it purchased at 2284 West and 3500 South Streets. As the congregation grew, Rev. Warren Sechler became its full-time minister. A new building, shown here on the day of dedication services, was constructed at 2600 West 3800 South Street on September 23, 1962. (DN.)

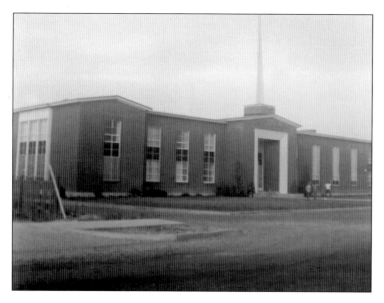

The LDS population of the area was also growing. Numerous new meetinghouses were constructed, including this chapel at 3270 West 3650 South Street. This building was dedicated in 1957, and initially housed Granger Ward, Granger Eighth Ward, and Granger Eleventh Ward. This is how the building looked in 1962. It was torn down in 2001. (WVCHS.)

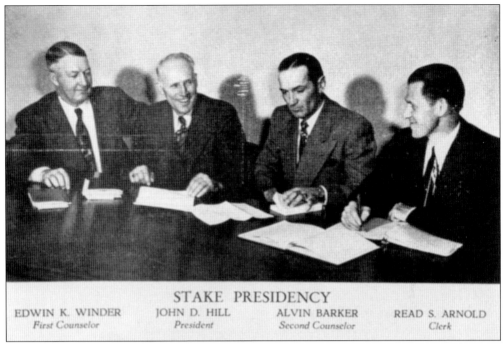

STAKE PRESIDENCY

EDWIN K. WINDER	JOHN D. HILL	ALVIN BARKER	READ S. ARNOLD
First Counselor	*President*	*Second Counselor*	*Clerk*

On January 12, 1947, the North Jordan Stake was created for the 4,644 Mormons in the area, including the following wards: Bennion (425 members), Granger First (922), Granger Second (915), Hunter (1,017), Redwood (540), and Taylorsville (825). They met in the Hunter Ward House. Their first stake president was John D. Hill, with counselors Edwin K. Winder and Alvin Barker, and Read S. Arnold as clerk. (WVCHS.)

On January 12, 1947, at a meeting in the Hunter Ward House, the North Jordan Stake was created for the 4,644 Mormons in the area, including the following wards: Bennion (425 members), Granger First (922), Granger Second (915), Hunter (1,017), Redwood (540), and Taylorsville (825). Their first stake president was John D. Hill, with counselors Edwin K. Winder and Alvin Barker, and Read S. Arnold as clerk. (WVCHS.)

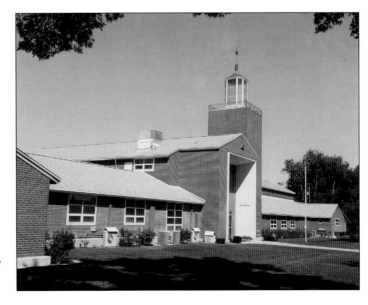

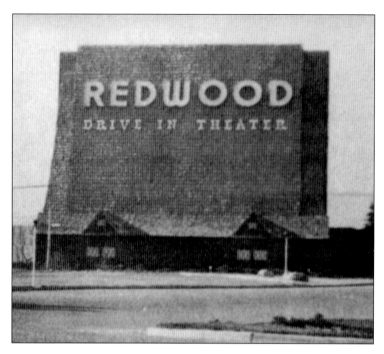

Built at 3700 South Redwood Road in 1949, the Redwood Drive-in Theater was the second of its kind in all of Salt Lake County. The drive-in was a $500,000-million investment and could accommodate 900 cars. As of 2011, it is still in operation. In 1956, another drive-in theater, Valley-Vu, opened at 4800 West and 3500 South Streets. (WVCHS.)

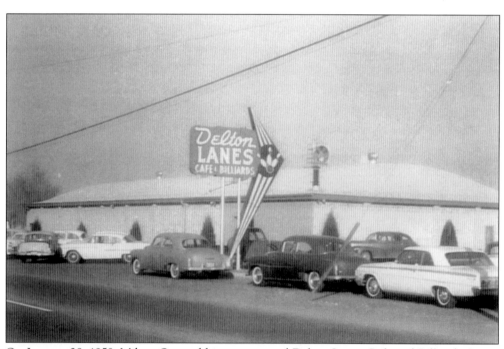

On January 28, 1958, Milton Orr and his sons opened Delton Lanes Café and Billiards. It was a $350,000 investment, sporting 12 bowling lanes, a snack bar, and complete facilities. Delton Lanes, located at 3455 South 3600 West Street, has remained a fixture in the community ever since. It is pictured here on opening day. (WVCHS.)

Stanley and Myrl Todd opened a roller-skating rink at 1700 West 3500 South Street but sold the building to Mickey McMillan for use as a dance pavilion in 1944. Their new S&M Roller Skating Rink, shown here, opened at 3950 South Redwood Road. It was popular for decades with school and church groups. (WVCHS.)

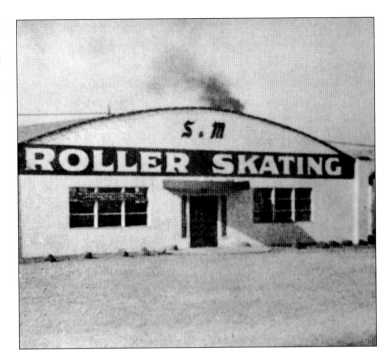

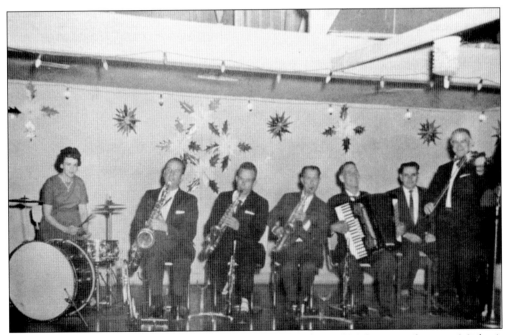

After Mickey McMillan bought the old roller-skating rink in 1944, he turned it into Mickey's Danceland, which held dances every Saturday night. A player of the violin since grade school, Mickey organized his own orchestra to provide the music at the hall. From left to right are Phyllis Barton, Bert Barton, Lloyd Martin, Wilford Webb, Bert Owen, LaVerne Dickson, and Mickey McMillan. (WVCHS.)

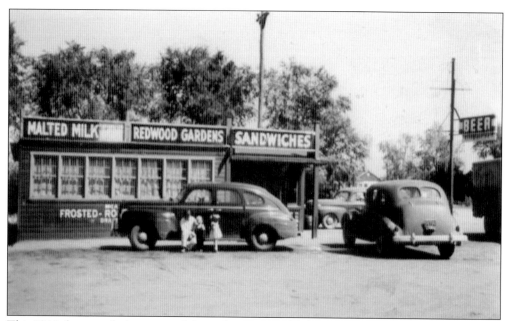

This 1946 photograph shows one of the early eating establishments in the area—a root beer stand called Redwood Gardens on the northwest corner of Redwood Road and 3500 South Street. Started by Frank Erath, the stand grew to include milk shakes and sandwiches on its menu. The establishment was sold in 1939 to O. Thayne Acord, his first of many business ventures in Granger. (WVCHS.)

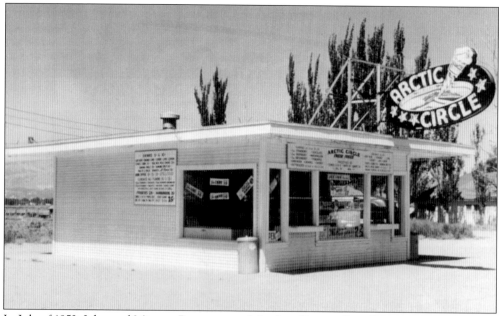

In July of 1952, John and Mignon Roper opened the first "drive-in" in Granger—Roper's Arctic Circle at 2200 West 3500 South Street. "Jack and Min's" was a popular place to get a foot-long hotdog, a juicy hamburger, or a chocolate-coated, ice cream cone known as a "brown topper," until the establishment closed in 1970. A new Arctic Circle was built at 4073 West 4100 South Street. (WVCHS.)

50

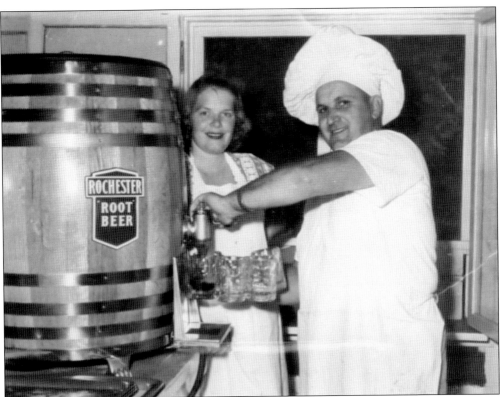

Ab and Dot Beutler opened Ab's Drive-in in Hunter at 5419 West 3500 South Street in 1951. The Beutlers are shown above brewing their homemade root beer in a 1953 photograph. Also shown is the original restaurant in the early 1950s. The original menu included steaks, homemade pies, and the signature "Fat Boy" hamburger. In 1992, the Beutlers opened a second location in Kearns. Both locations were closed 11 years later, opening a larger restaurant between the two restaurants at 4591 South 5600 West Street. The Beutlers' son Bart and his wife, Elizabeth, run the new Ab's Drive-in. (WVCHS.)

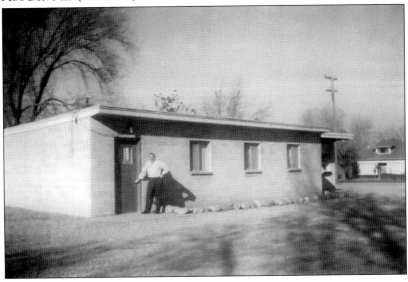

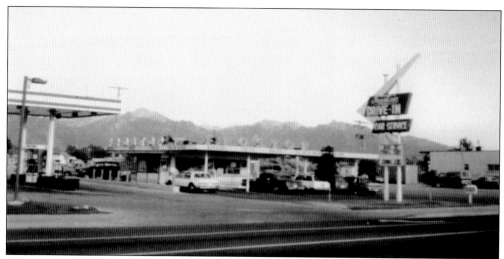

In 1926, L.S. Harvey started the first Frostop Root Beer stand in Springfield, Ohio. In the 1950s, dozens opened across America, including one on 3510 South 3600 West Street in what would become West Valley. Their brown and yellow neon signs were icons of the 1950's—the company peaked in 1958. This photograph shows West Valley Frostop's final day in business, August 30, 1994. (WVCHS.)

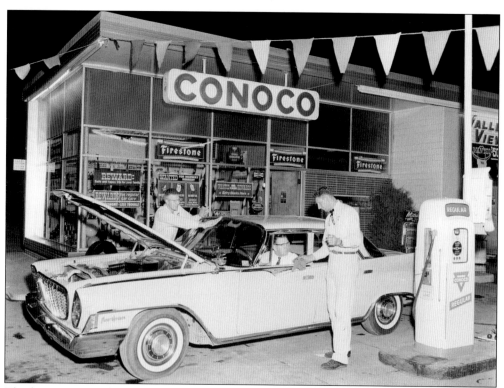

The first gas station in the area was opened by Chris Anast in 1917 at 1989 West and 3500 South Streets. At the time, this was the only gas station between State Street and Magna. Later, more gas stations opened up, including this Conoco service station at 4000 West and 3500 South Streets, seen here in this May 1962 photograph. (USHS.)

Nile T. Mackay ran a service station at the northeast corner of Redwood Road and 3500 South Street, shown here in this 1954 photograph. As the automobile grew in popularity, so did service stations. The West Valley area had 23 service stations by 1963. Mackay, part of a longtime Granger family, was also one of the 41 men who formed the Granger Lions Club on March 27, 1948. (WVCHS.)

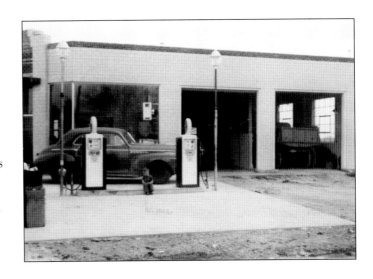

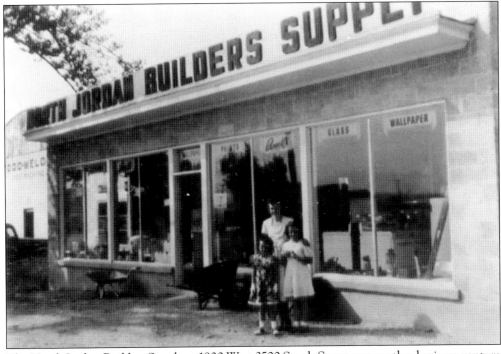

The North Jordan Builders Supply at 1900 West 3500 South Street was another business venture of O. Thayne Acord's. It operated as such from 1947 to 1958, when it changed its name to the Granger Builders Supply. West of this business was the Todd Welding and Machine Company (later called TWAMCO), which was started in 1936 by brothers Fred and Edgar Todd. (WVCHS.)

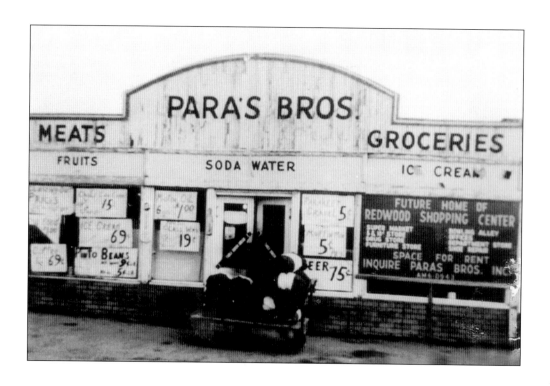

In 1945, Paras brothers John, Chris, and Gus started a grocery business on the southeast corner of 3500 South Redwood Road, shown above in this 1947 photograph. The business expanded into the Model City Market, a large shopping center for its day that included a café, health studio, hardware, groceries, furniture, and automobile parts. John Paras Furniture expanded to the south of this development and incorporated in 1961. Fifty years later, John Paras Furniture had grown from these humble beginnings to four locations in two states. (Both, WVCHS.)

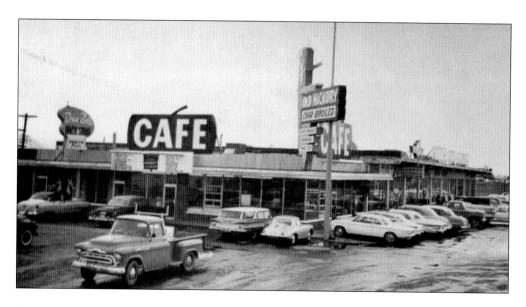

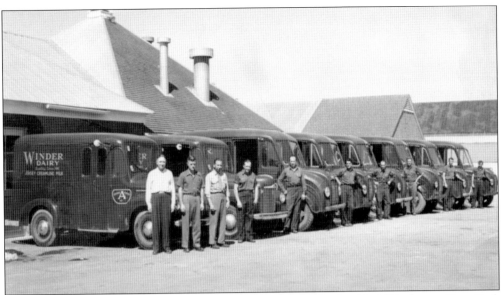

This 1950 photograph shows (from left to right) George Winder, Ned Winder, unidentified, Newell Foulks, Dale Petersen, Hiat Ashby, Brig Smith, Orm Coulam, Marv Wallace, and Richard Winder standing outside the Winder Dairy in front of the company's delivery trucks. At the end of World War II, they had 12 routes and six drivers. By 1960, they had 80 routes with 40 drivers and were Utah's largest home delivery dairy. (Courtesy Winder Farms.)

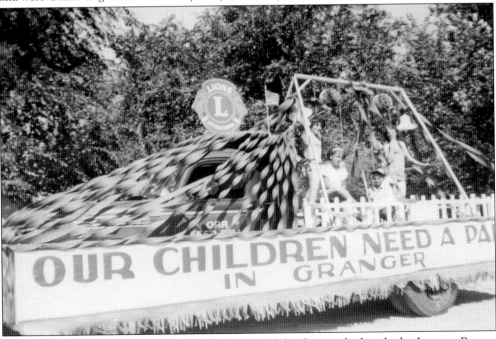

After 1947, Granger and Hunter each had Lions Clubs that worked with the Jaycees, Rotary Clubs, and the chamber of commerce to promote the area. Working with the Woodbury family, they built Granger Park in 1954, shown here being promoted in the Days of '47 Parade. They held Miss Granger pageants, worked to get bus service to the area, and were early advocates for incorporation. (Courtesy Bill Barton.)

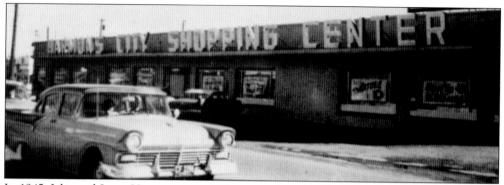

In 1945, Jake and Irene Harmon started Harmon's City Shopping Center, which is located at 3995 West 3500 South Street. The forerunner to Harmon's grocery store was the Market Spot, which they opened at 3300 South Main Street in 1932. In 1971, the original Harmon's shown in this photograph caught fire and burned to the ground, but the family pressed on and built a new Harmon's supermarket in its stead. (WVCHS.)

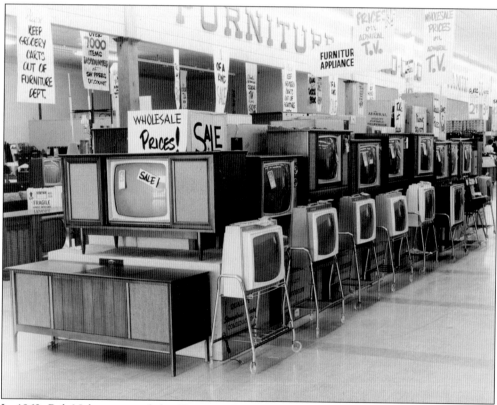

In 1962, Bob Nelson opened the Shopper's Discount Store on 1500 West 3500 South Street. What began as a 7,000-square-foot store with four employees grew to a 60,000-square-foot store with 140 employees in its first 3.5 years. The store sold a variety of goods, including groceries, furniture, and electronics, as seen in this 1966 photograph. (USHS.)

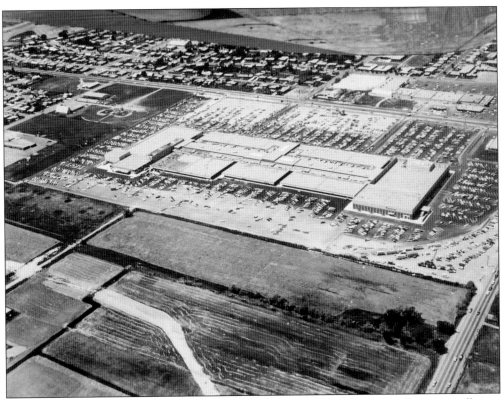

This aerial July 1970 photograph of Valley Fair Mall shows Utah's newest indoor shopping mall open for business. On the lower right corner of the photograph is 3500 South Street. 2700 West Street runs directly west of the mall, with a shopping center west of it where city hall would be built in 1990. In the upper left quadrant are the original Granger Elementary and the original Granger Community Christian Church. In the foreground, empty land would soon become the I-215 freeway. This segment of the freeway was built beginning in 1973 and completed in November 1976. The image of the center court of the new mall was also taken in July 1970 when the mall opened. (Both, DN.)

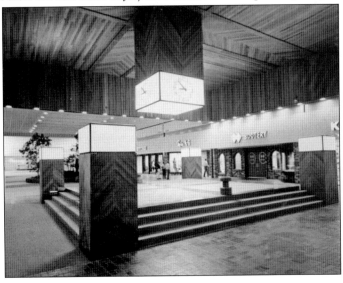

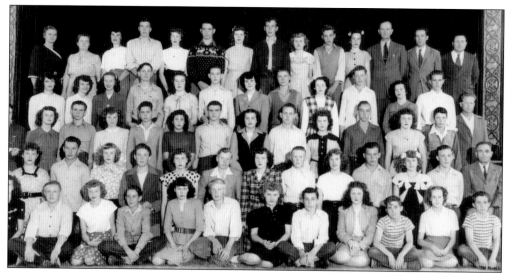

Pictured are Monroe School's ninth-graders from their junior high school program in 1947. Monroe had junior high classes from around 1910 until 1949, when Valley Junior High School was built at 4195 South 3200 West Street. With local grade schools dissolving their junior high programs, 550 students entered Valley for its inaugural 1949–1950 school year with Claude C. Lemon as the first principal. (WVCHS.)

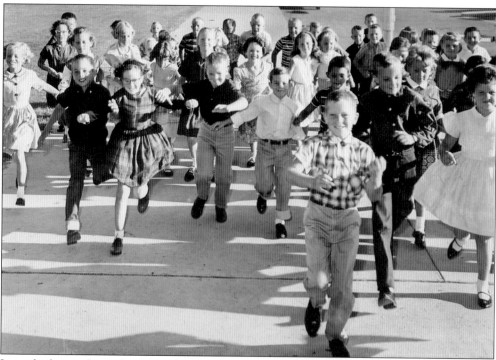

Long shadows indicate that it is early morning as Hillsdale Elementary School students rush to the first day of school in August 1963. Hillsdale opened in September 1961 at 3275 West 3100 South Street, and with the booming growth of Granger in the 1960s, it was already at an enrollment of 975 in its first year. Other schools, such as Redwood Elementary (1953) and Granger Elementary (1956) opened a few years earlier. (DN.)

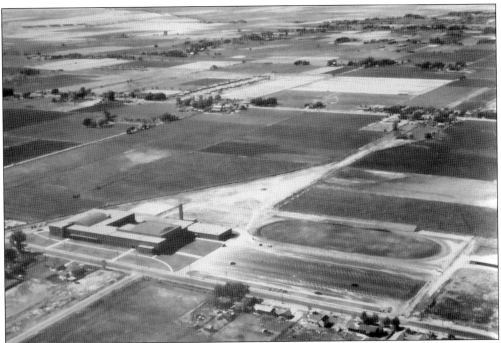

This aerial photograph of the new Granger High School campus in 1958 shows a largely rural area. A future Bangerter Highway would run along the high school immediately to the west. Trees and homes mark where 4000 West Street, 4400 West Street, 4800 West Street, 5200 West Street, and so forth run as the scene stretches into Hunter, with 4100 South Street at the top of the view. (Courtesy Gwen Winder.)

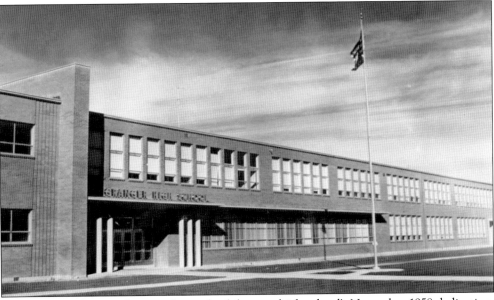

This photograph was taken on the week of the new high school's November 1958 dedication. Granger High School took two years to build at a cost of $1,628,000. Originally, it had 36 classrooms and was intended to accommodate 1,035 students. Classes for the first few months were held in unfinished and often unfurnished rooms. The first principal was Gibb R. Madsen. (DN.)

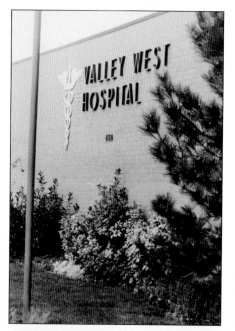

The first hospital on the west side of the Salt Lake Valley was the Valley West Hospital built at 4160 West 3500 South Street. The original building cost $500,000 and included only 40 beds and three operating rooms. It did, however, offer surgery, emergency, maternity, nursing, X-ray, laboratory, and physical therapy services. Ground was broken in September 1962. Below, community leaders Edwin K. Winder (left) and Estel Wright cut the ribbon on July 22, 1963. As the medical needs in the area grew, so did the hospital. A new hospital facility built on the original site in 1981 replaced the old building and was renamed the Pioneer Valley Hospital. (Both, DN.)

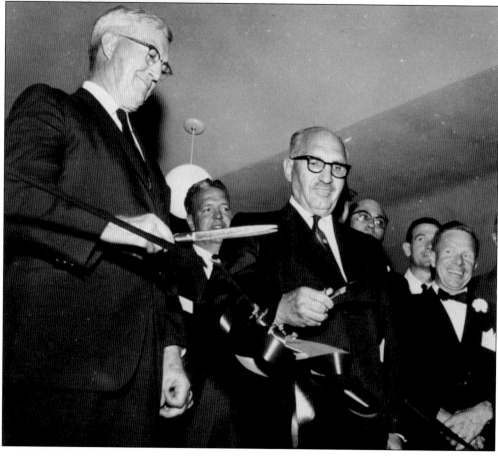

Four

A New City is Born
1976–1982

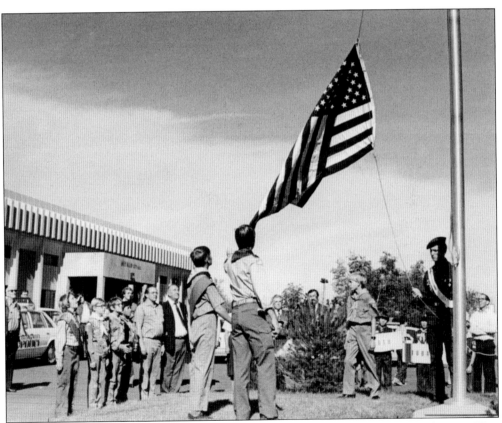

On October 29, 1980, Boy Scouts raise the American flag at the dedication of the new West Valley City Hall while Mayor Hank Price and Commissioners Renee Mackay and Jerry Wagstaff look on. After a previous failed attempt, the incorporation vote passed by just 72 votes (less than one percent). This photograph represents a new day dawning as Utah's newest city is born! (Photograph by Howard C. Moore; courtesy DN.)

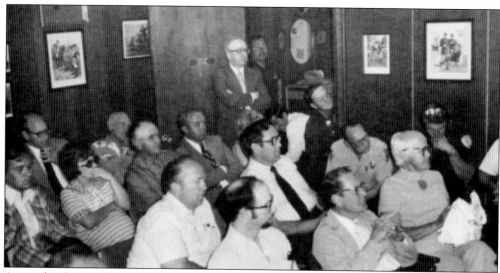

A crowd gathers in Henry "Hank" Price's office of the justice of the peace at 3460 South Redwood Road during a Granger-Hunter Community Council meeting to discuss incorporation. A former community council chairman and Granger Lions Club president, Price was the driving force behind incorporation and would accentuate points with the frequent waves of his unlit cigar. The Granger-Hunter Community Council was formed in 1964. (WVCHS.)

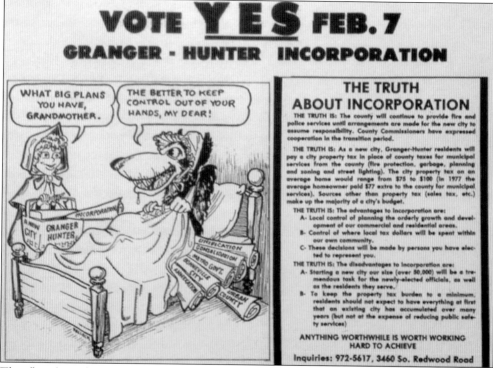

This flyer from the 1978 incorporation effort advocates a city. An amazing 47 percent of voters turned out to defeat the measure 6,053 to 4,944. But a new effort was soon begun, which sought to better educate voters. Voters approved the incorporation of West Valley City by a vote of 5,185 to 5,113 on March 7, 1980. (WVCHS.)

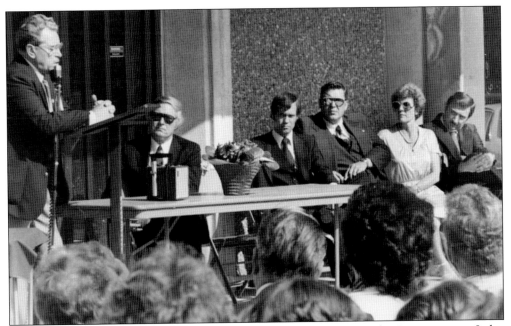

Mayor Henry H. Price gives his inaugural remarks after being sworn in by Granger native Judge David K. Winder (seated left). Judge Bruce Larsen, city auditor M. Gerry Ashman, and city commissioners Renee W. Mackay and Jerald L. Wagstaff are also sworn in on July 1, 1980—the city's birthday. (Courtesy W. Claudell Johnson, DN.)

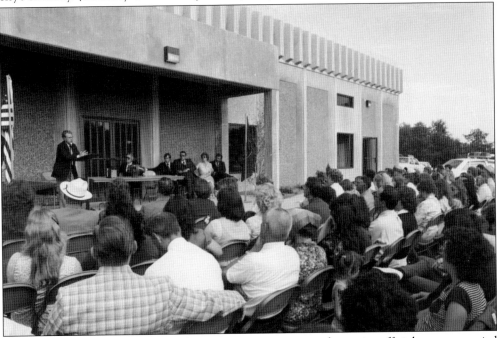

As the crowd gathered outside for the swearing in ceremony of new city officials, many worried about the disincorporation vote that was to be held July 8. "West Valley City should be smothered in its creaking crib," declared the *Salt Lake Tribune*. But an astounding 15,781 turned out to vote, and 58.5 percent voted to keep the city. (DN.)

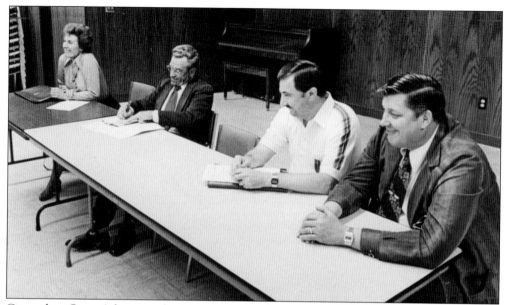

City auditor Gerry Ashman, right, joins city leaders Renee Mackay, Hank Price, and Jerry Wagstaff in one of the first city commission meetings. The early days were tough, and the mayor and commissioners paid for gas for the police cars out of their own pockets until the new city could get financing. A loan from Zions Bank allowed them to meet the first payroll on July 10. (DN.)

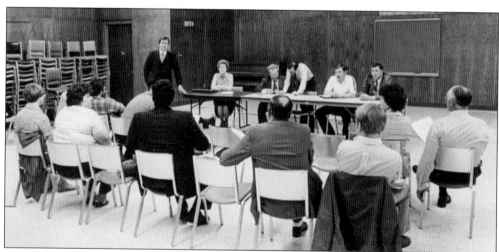

Early matters tackled by the West Valley City Commission included renaming 3650 South Street "Lancer Way," entering a float in the Days of '47 Parade, forging contracts for services with neighboring cities and the county, and creating a short-lived Commission on Public Decency that would screen every R-rated movie shown in the city, especially those at the Valley-Vu Drive-in. (DN.)

On October 29, 1980, Commissioner Renee Mackay, Mayor Hank Price, and Commissioner Jerry Wagstaff prepare to cut the ribbon on city hall, a remodeled building at 2470 South Redwood Road. Much of the furnishings and equipment had been donated by area businesses, and open house activities for the community were held throughout the day. (DN.)

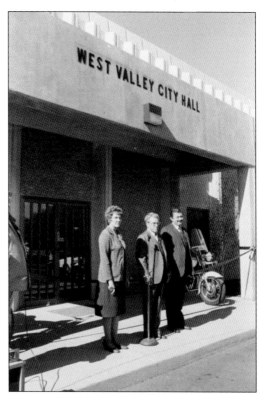

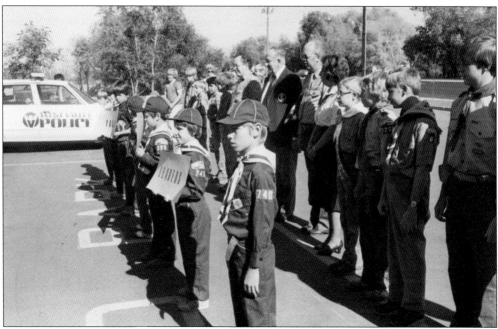

Area Cub Scouts and Boy Scouts are excited to be at the new city hall. One of the new police cars is visible in the background. The first case of the new police department was a lost boy—two-year-old George Robert Walk. Officers Bill McCarthy and Brent Bracken found the boy toddling around the intersection of 3500 South and 3200 West Streets and returned him home safely. (DN.)

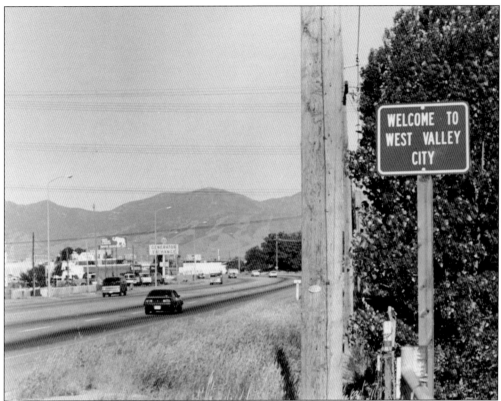

This sign greets motorists heading west towards the Oquirrh Mountains after crossing the Jordan River at 3300 South Street. The first official city marker, it was proudly installed in the first week of the city despite the looming disincorporation vote of July 8. The new city purchased 25 of the signs from the Utah State Prison for $273.50. (Photograph by Jack Monson; courtesy DN.)

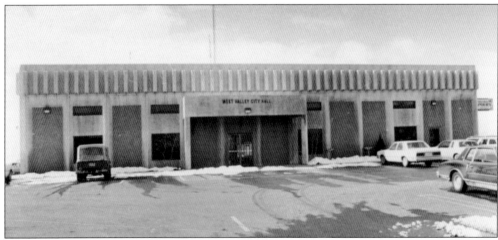

Rented by the city at first, the original city hall was purchased in 1981 by the city's new Municipal Building Authority. When city leaders learned in 1984 that it would take over $200,000 in retrofits to bring city hall into compliance with the new American with Disabilities Act, they began considering building a new city hall. (DN.)

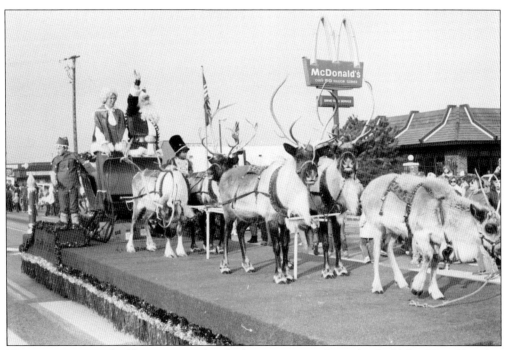

The new city enjoyed a Christmas parade, which was put on each year by the Valley West Chamber of Commerce (later known as Chamber West). Santa Claus would be the climax of the parade as he followed the procession down 3500 South to the Valley Fair Mall. For many years, children were delighted to see Santa accompanied by live reindeer. (DN.)

In 1980, residents saw what was then the highest building in the west side of the valley as the five-story Midwest Office Plaza took shape on the southwest corner of 3500 South and 4000 West Streets. F. Ray Green and Terry Harmon were the owners of the building, which used several floors for the corporate headquarters of Harmon's grocery business. (DN.)

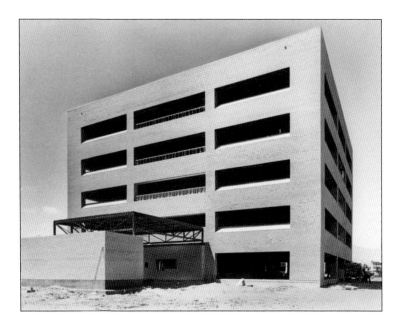

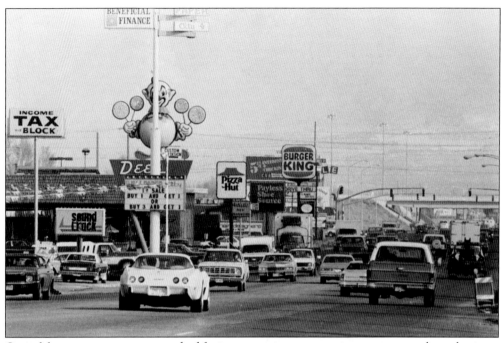

One of the reasons proponents pushed for incorporation was to gain greater control over business development. This 1980 photograph of 3500 South Street looking east near Market Street shows the evolution of the area's main street under Salt Lake County's loose development rules. (DN.)

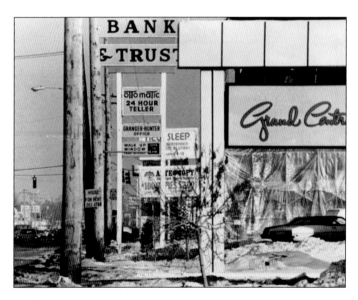

This 1978 photograph of 3500 South Street looking east near 4000 West Street illustrates some of the urban sprawl issues argued about among incorporation proponents. University of Utah planning classes would take field trips to 3500 South Street to demonstrate poor examples of urban planning. New city leaders worked to improve the look of 3500 South Street—a process that took decades. (DN.)

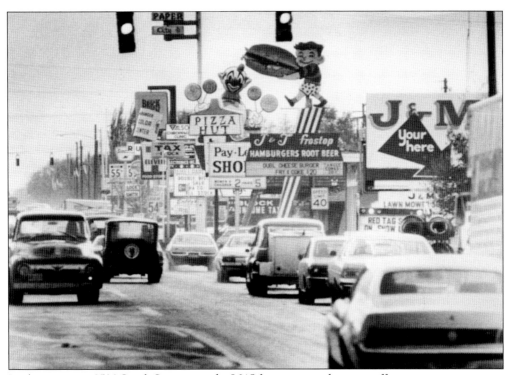

Looking west on 3500 South Street near the I-215 freeway interchange, traffic continues to increase in Utah's newest city. With 60,000 people at incorporation, West Valley City was Utah's third largest city. It continued to grow in the 1980s, bringing more urban challenges. (DN.)

But not all of the new West Valley City was suburbanized when it incorporated. This February 1980 image shows a relatively rural Granger. However, farm scenes like this continued to disappear from the landscape as new subdivisions were built and roads widened. The area still boasted relatively affordable housing with minor commutes. (DN.)

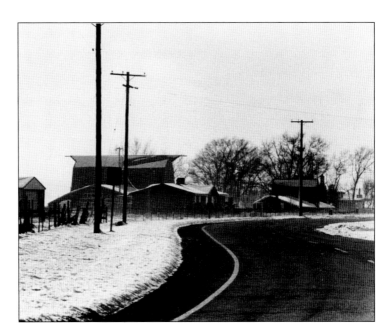

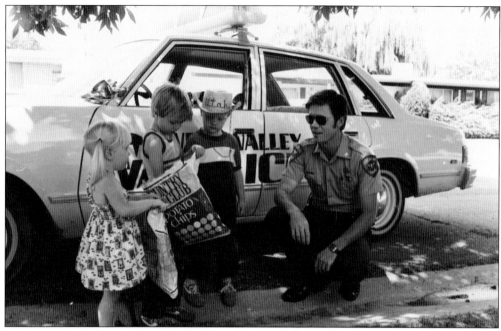

On August 13, 1980, West Valley City police sergeant Tom McLachlan patrols city streets and pauses to visit with children while on duty in his new squad car. This photograph was taken as part of a news story explaining how the city was building its police department from the ground up. There were 45 police officers sworn in on the day the city was born, with plans (as funds permitted) to increase the number of officers to 63. New police chief David Campbell worked quickly to build a respectable force, obtain police cars, and order guns and bullets. Residents appreciated that 10 or 11 officers were on patrol during weekend evenings, compared to just four or five sheriff's deputies before incorporation. (Both, photograph by Jack Monson; courtesy DN.)

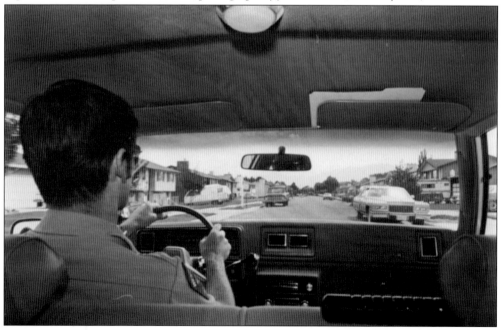

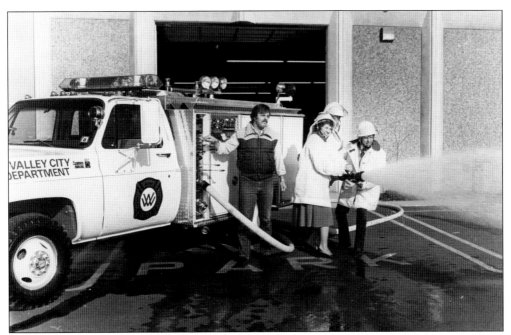

On January 1, 1981, the new city's contracts expired with Salt Lake County for fire protection, planning and zoning, and public works. A 6.5-percent franchise tax went into place the same day, allowing West Valley City to provide its own services. City firefighter Condon Hansen helps Mayor Price and Commissioners Mackay and Wagstaff celebrate by spraying the fire hose from one of the three new trucks. (DN.)

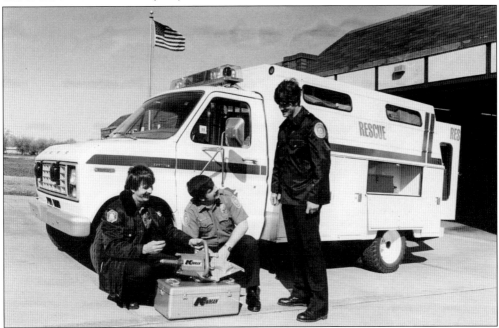

Firefighters at Station 72 (4324 West 4100 South Street) explore the equipment of their new vehicle, a 1980 Ford heavy rescue truck that the city bought for $18,000 in 1982. The truck was equipped with a generator for portable power and an air system for the fire crew's air packs. (DN.)

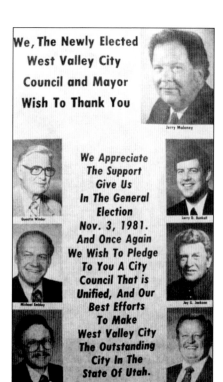

We, The Newly Elected West Valley City Council and Mayor Wish To Thank You

Jerry Maloney

Quentin Winder

Larry D. Bunkall

We Appreciate The Support Give Us In The General Election Nov. 3, 1981. And Once Again We Wish To Pledge To You A City Council That is Unified, And Our Best Efforts To Make West Valley City The Outstanding City In The State Of Utah.

Michael Embley

Jay G. Jackson

In February 1981, the city commission set up a task force to determine a better form of government. A recommendation for the council-manager form was approved on July 28 by a three-to-one margin (although only 11 percent of voters turned out). Gerald Maloney was elected the city's second mayor. The first city council included Pete Winder, Michael Embley, Claude Jones, Larry Bunkall, Jay Jackson, and Brent Anderson. (WVCHS.)

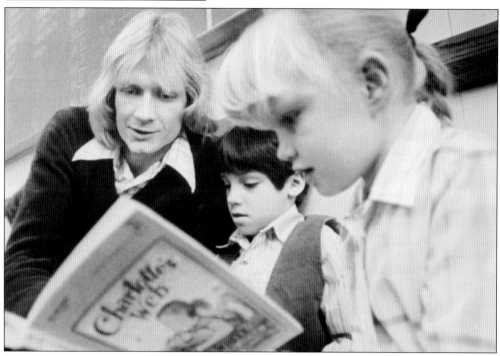

The growing city included many young families. On February 19, 1982, Ron Woolf, a second-grade teacher at Douglas T. Orchard Elementary School (6744 West and 3800 South Street), helps Joe Crandall and Ann Pearce with their reading skills. (Photograph by Gerald W. Silver; courtesy DN.)

Five

BECOMING A
FIRST-CLASS CITY
1983–1996

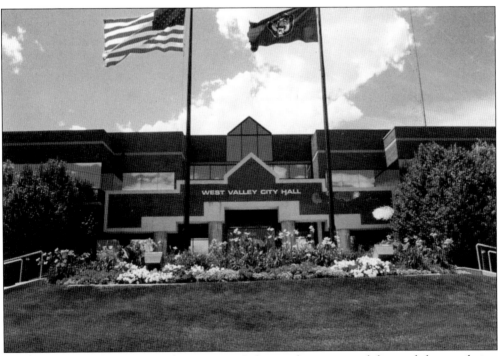

The 1980s and early 1990s saw the young city's financial situation stabilize and the population grow. The city of 72,509 at incorporation in 1980 had grown to 100,000 by 1996, when Utah governor Mike Leavitt declared West Valley City one of Utah's "first-class cities." In those years, the Hercules area was annexed in 1988, and a new city hall was dedicated in 1990. (KC.)

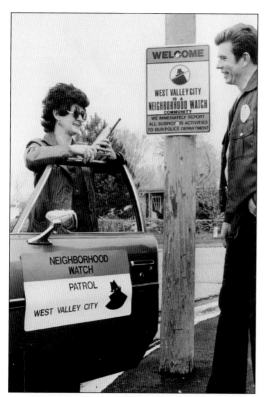

In April 1983, police chief David C. Campbell (right) began a pilot program for Neighborhood Watch. The program had 30 volunteers in one neighborhood, including watch leader Carma Allred (left). In the years ahead, the program would grow to include 94 neighborhoods, and West Valley City would consistently win national awards for their Night Out Against Crime events. (Photograph by Jack Monson; courtesy DN.)

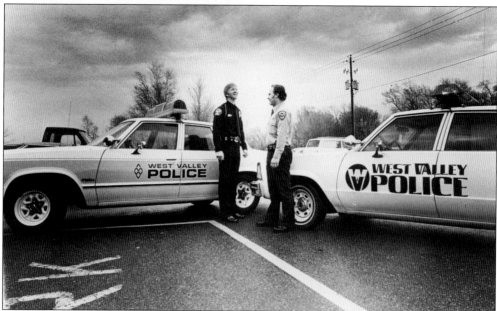

In May 1983, the West Valley City Police Department replaced the tan and brown uniforms (in use since incorporation) with navy blue ones. Shoulder patches designed by officers were upgraded, as were the color and look of patrol cars. Chief Campbell said the changes were part of an effort to show that they were becoming a professional organization. (Photograph by Jack Monson; courtesy DN.)

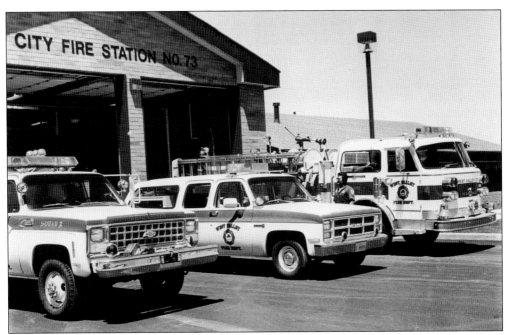

In July 1984, the West Valley City Fire Department moved into a new station at 2834 South 2700 West Street. Known as Station 73, the new facility was later joined by Station 74 (5545 West 3100 South Street) and Station 75 (3660 South 1950 West Street). Previous stations were also located at 4160 South and 6400 West Streets (Station 71) and 4314 West 4100 South Street (Station 72). (Photograph by Steve Fidel; courtesy DN.)

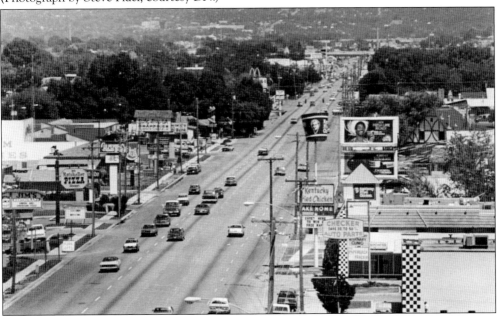

As the city's fifth birthday approached in the summer of 1985, city staff put together a plan to better control development on 3500 South Street. This photograph shows east 3500 South Street in June. A few years later Bangerter Highway would slice through, just east of the Kentucky Fried Chicken. (Photograph by Paul Barker; courtesy DN.)

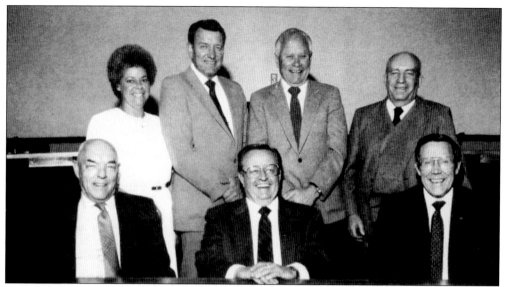

As it appeared in 1989, the fourth city council included, from left to right, (first row) Carrol Elford, Mayor Brent Anderson, and Gearld Wright; (second row) Janice Fisher, Leland DeLange, Duane Moss, and Gordon Evans. Anderson became the city's fourth mayor on May 20, 1987, after being appointed to replace Mayor Michael Embley, who had resigned. He was later elected in his own right and served until January 1994. (WVCHS.)

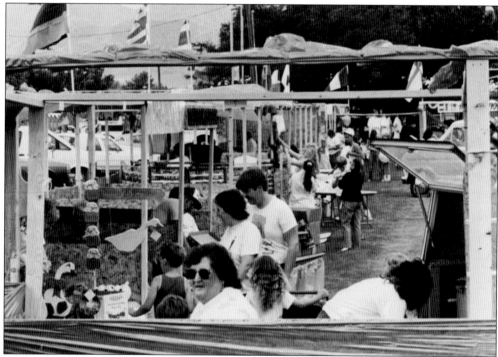

Started in 1981, West Valley Days commemorated the city's incorporation and involved just a few hundred participants. In 1983, it was renamed the WestFest International Festival. It continued to grow, featuring foods from around the world in a food court setting, live performances, and fireworks. This photograph shows WestFest in 1989. (Photograph by Don Grayston; courtesy DN.)

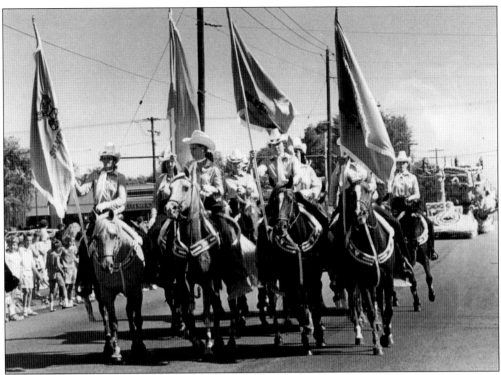

In 1988, WestFest had an "Old West" theme, complete with mountain men, teepees, and blacksmith demonstrations. The parade that year had 80 entries, including floats, bands, and horses. Traditionally held the last weekend in June, WestFest has grown to involve tens of thousands of people each year. (Photograph by Paul Barker; courtesy DN.)

Children scramble after saltwater taffy tossed at the crowd during the annual WestFest parade in 1990. Elaborate floats, skateboarders, Corvettes, politicians, and Girl Scouts were among the many entries that year. During the first 15 years, WestFest was held at Granger Park at 3600 West and 3500 South Streets. (Photograph by Gerald Silver; courtesy DN.)

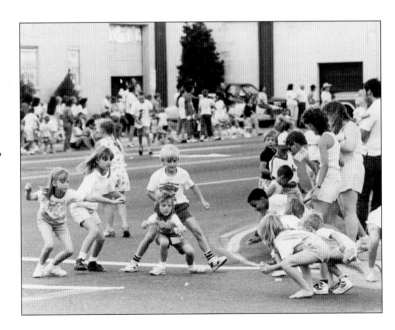

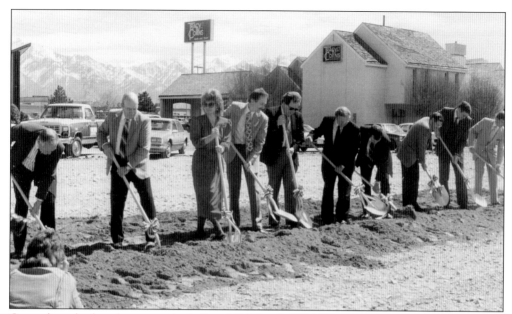

Ground was broken for a new city hall at 3600 South 2700 West Street on April 5, 1988. From left to right are council members Duane Moss and Gordon Evans, city recorder Karen Leftwich, council member Claude Jones, former mayor Jerry Maloney, Mayor Brent Anderson, council members Leland DeLange and Gearld Wright, city manager John Newman, and unidentified. Newman served from 1982 to 1991. (WVCHS.)

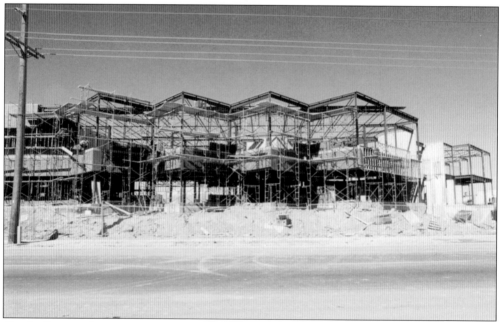

City hall was under construction as part of a larger civic complex that included a justice court. At the ground-breaking ceremony, Utah Supreme Court Associate Chief Justice I. Daniel Stewart commented that the new facility would give the city "a new sense of identity" that did not exist in "a prefab warehouse unit that also isn't exactly conducive to the dignified conduct of judicial proceedings." (WVCHS.)

Located west across 2700 West Street from Valley Fair Mall, the new city hall was intended to be the beginning of a true city center for West Valley City. In 1987, the year of the bicentennial of the US Constitution, 2700 West Street was renamed Constitution Boulevard, adding dignity to the new city hall's address. (WVCHS.)

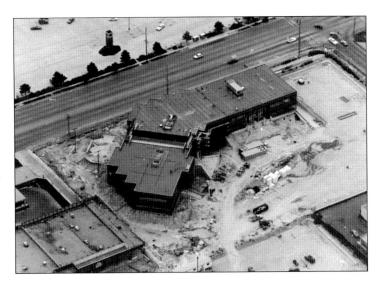

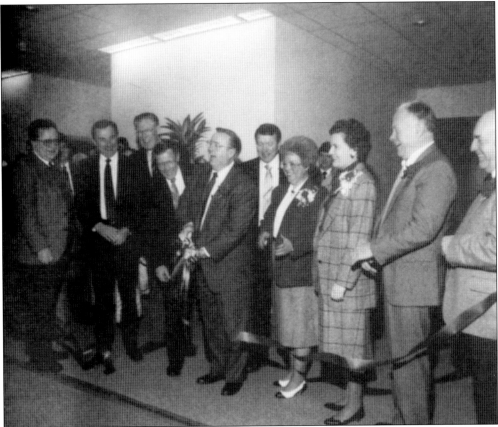

The new $9.6 million city hall officially opened on January 2, 1990. From left to right are former mayor Gerald Maloney, former commissioner Jerald Wagstaff, Governor Bangerter's local government liaison Doug Bischoff, council member Gearld Wright, Mayor Brent Anderson, and council members Leland DeLange, Janice Fisher, Margaret Peterson, Duane Moss, and Gordon Evans. The Granger High School band and jazz choir provided music for the festivities. (WVCHS.)

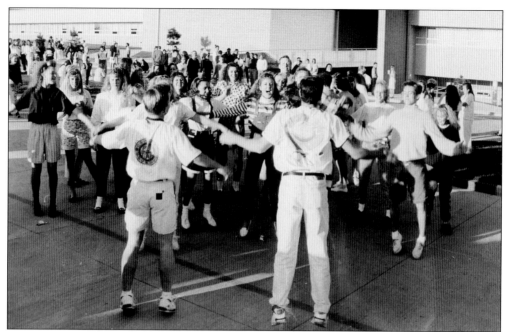

The city received their second high school when Hunter High School opened for the 1990–1991 school year. Located at 4200 South 5600 West Street, the school was evacuated on October 4, 1991, due to a gas leak. Students are seen doing jumping jacks to keep warm during their cool hour outside the "Home of the Wolverines." (DN.)

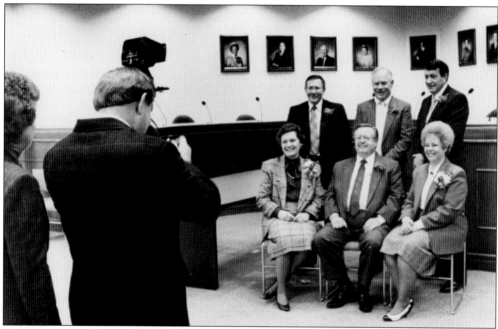

On January 2, 1990, city officials pose for a group shot in the new city council chambers on the day new officials were sworn in and city hall officially opened. From left to right are (first row) Margaret Peterson, Mayor Brent Anderson, and Janice Fisher; (second row) Gearld Wright, Duane Moss, and Leland DeLange. (Photograph by Gerald W. Silver; courtesy DN.)

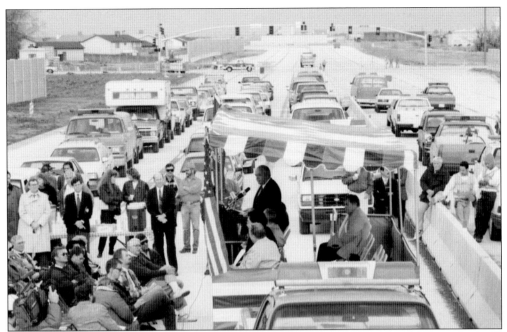

On November 26, 1991, Utah governor Norm Bangerter dedicated the first section of the West Valley Highway (between 2100 South and 3500 South Streets). A West Valley City native, Governor Bangerter had helped procure over $40 million of state funds for the highway. In May 1993, the Utah Transportation Commission renamed the road Bangerter Highway in his honor. (Photograph by Ravell Call; courtesy DN.)

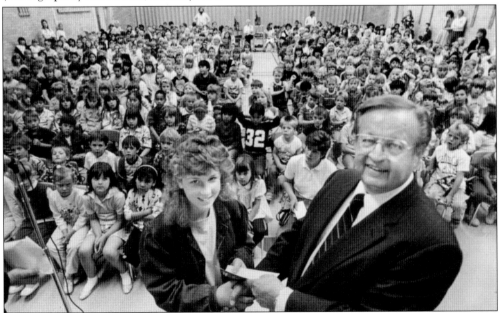

Mayor Brent Anderson presented a $400 check to student president Christy Starr at an assembly at Stansbury Elementary on May 6, 1988. Stansbury won the "Looking Good" clean-up campaign award for the second year in a row. Students collected 160 large bags of trash, more than any of the other 18 participating elementary schools. (Photograph by Don Grayston; courtesy DN.)

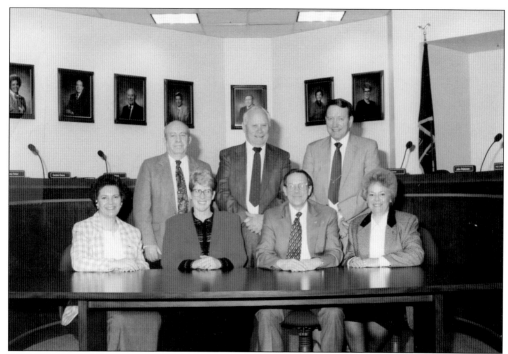

In November 1993, Gearld Wright was elected West Valley City's fifth mayor over state senator Bill Barton. In January 1994, the makeup of the city council was as follows: from left to right, (first row) Margaret Peterson, Barbara Thomas, Mayor Gearld Wright, and Janice Fisher; (second row) Gordon Evans, Duane Moss, and Leland DeLange. Wright would be elected an unprecedented three times. (WVCHS.)

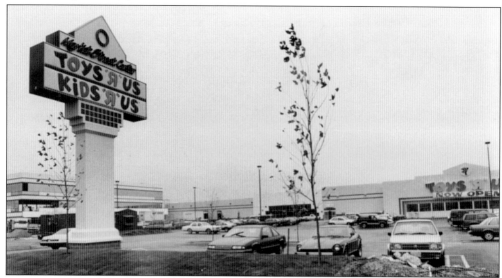

Initially, city hall was going to be built at Granger Park. Market Street was the preferred location, however, because the city hall could then serve as an anchor for development. With the city hall in place, a second redevelopment area was created, and tax incentives were provided to help make the new Market Street Center attractive for new businesses such as Toys "R" Us, shown here on its opening day. (Photograph by Don Grayston; courtesy DN.)

Six

OLYMPIC DREAMS
1997–2002

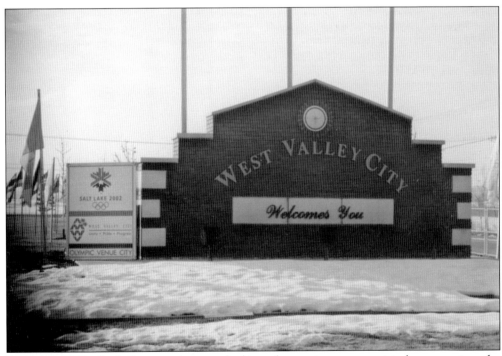

In the late 1990s, Eagle Scout projects resulted in welcome signs at two critical gateways into the city—Michael Lang did one at Bangerter Highway just south of 2100 South Street and Douglas Honsvick did one at 4100 South Street just west of the Jordan River. The signage into the city became even more significant as the 2002 Winter Olympic Games neared. This was a time of great growth and maturity for the city. It was a season of Olympic dreams. (KC.)

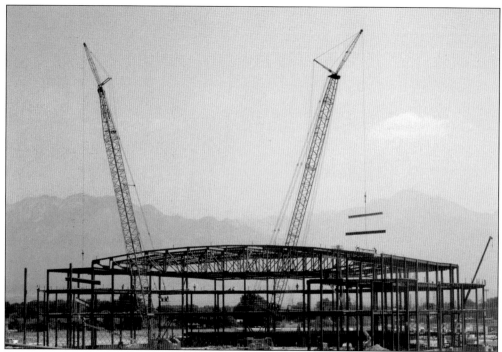

On July 6, 1995, Mayor Gearld Wright announced that the Denver Grizzlies professional hockey team would be relocating to a new 10,000-seat arena to be built in West Valley City. The city also began lobbying for the new arena to be an Olympic venue for the upcoming 2002 Winter Games. Ground was broken on March 22, 1996. (KC.)

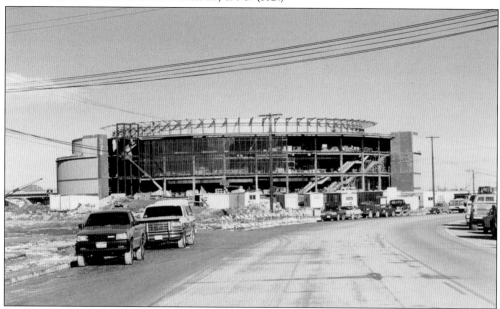

The new event center began taking shape in an empty field at 3200 South Decker Lake Drive. HOK, one of the world's premiere arena architects, designed the state-of-the-art facility. The arena would have the flexibility to accommodate 3,700 to 12,000 spectators. The building is 300,000 square feet on a 30-acre site. (KC.)

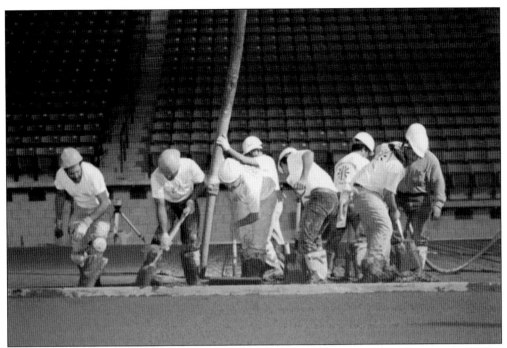

Taken on July 9, 1997, this image shows the concrete floor of the event center being poured. The overall construction of the building cost $54.1 million. Lance Blackwood of the city's economic development office helped oversee the construction of the building, which was built by Turner Construction. With no naming rights deals agreed upon, the city called the new event center the E-Center. (Photograph by Ravell Call; courtesy DN.)

To the northeast, 2,300 parking spaces are visible in the E-Center lot. On the left is I-215, providing major visibility for the new arena, with 3100 South Street flying over the freeway to connect to the E-Center's north side. Decker Lake Drive winds past the arena north into the Lake Pointe Business Park, with Decker Lake visible. The Salt Lake City skyline appears on the upper right. (KC.)

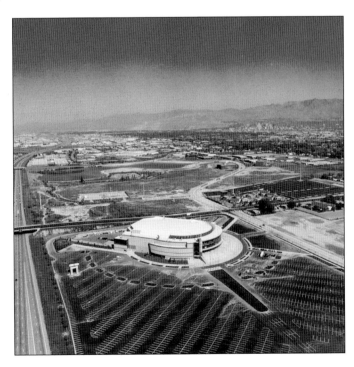

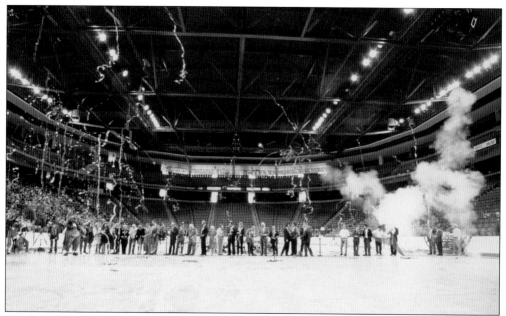

On Friday, September 19, 1997, dignitaries release giant poppers of confetti on the ice as the ribbon was cut on the new E-Center. Salt Lake Organizing Committee CEO Frank Joklik said on the day of the ribbon cutting that it was "a tremendous achievement that will enhance the quality of life in this part of the valley." (KC.)

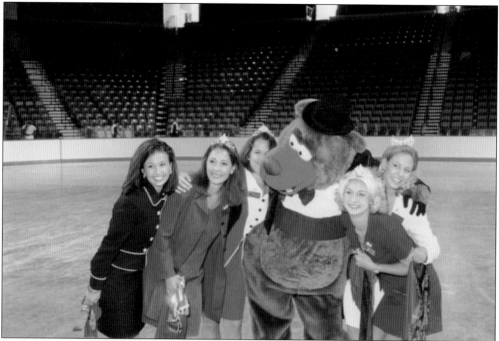

On September 19, 1997, Miss West Valley City and her attendants surround Grizbee, mascot to the new Utah Grizzlies. More than 2,000 community members turned out for the ribbon cutting of the new E-Center. In 1994, twenty-one-year-old Brooke Anderson was Miss West Valley City. She also won Miss Utah and went on to represent the state in the Miss America Pageant. (KC.)

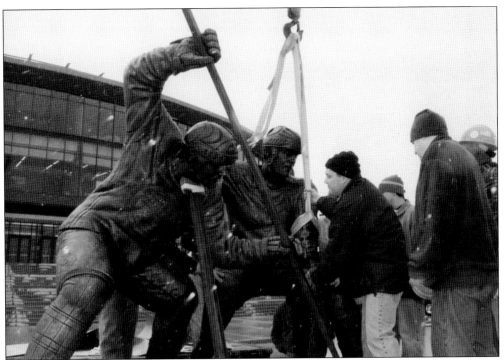

On January 15, 2002, just a few weeks before the Olympic Games would begin in Salt Lake, the bronze sculpture *Striving for Excellence* was installed in front of the E-Center. Sculpted by artist Stan Watts, the hockey players are 1.5 times life size and welcome visitors coming for the Olympics, Utah Grizzlies hockey games, or any other event. (KC.)

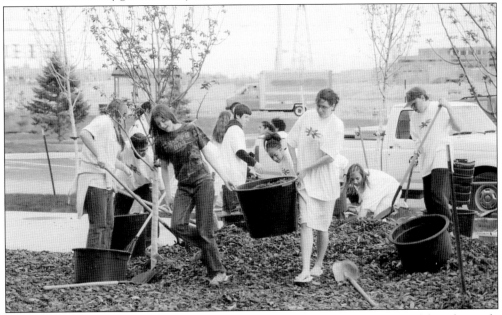

As part of the city's annual Youth Pride Day, young volunteers came to spread mulch at the newly landscaped E-Center. The E-Center was not only home of the Utah Grizzlies but also hosted concerts such as Neil Diamond, Elton John, and Janet Jackson. (KC.)

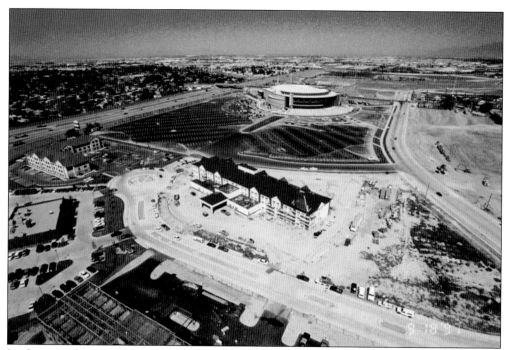

Looking north towards the E-Center, new hotels are under construction, including the Baymont Inn, Crystal Inn, and Country Inn & Suites. The newly opened Cracker Barrel restaurant is seen on the left, and open fields east of the E-Center would soon be filled with the Hollywood Connection arcades and movies and Hale Centre Theatre. (KC.)

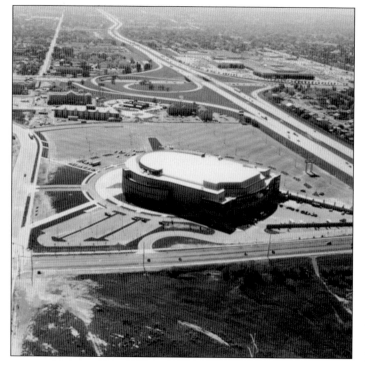

Looking south beyond the E-Center, the cloverleaf interchange of 3500 South Street and Interstate 215 is visible. Valley Fair Mall is southwest of the interchange. Stretching into the horizon east of I-215 is 2200 West Street. City events coordinator Kevin Conde took these aerial photographs when Tom Rehtberg flew him over the city in the Utah highway patrol helicopter. (KC.)

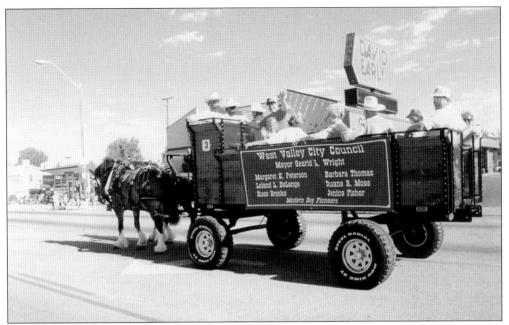

In 1997, Utah was celebrating the 150th anniversary of the arrival of Mormon pioneers. City leaders billed themselves as modern-day pioneers for their entry into the annual WestFest parade. The city was excited about the new arena and to be a venue city for the upcoming Olympics. (KC.)

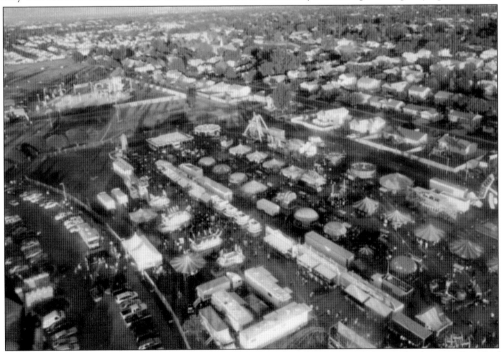

WestFest continued to be a favorite summer festival of tens of thousands on the last weekend of June, and had moved from Granger Park to Centennial Park. This aerial photograph shows the carnival to the southeast that had become part of the WestFest tradition. Salt Lake County's outdoor swimming pool and waterslide are visible just beyond the festivities. (KC.)

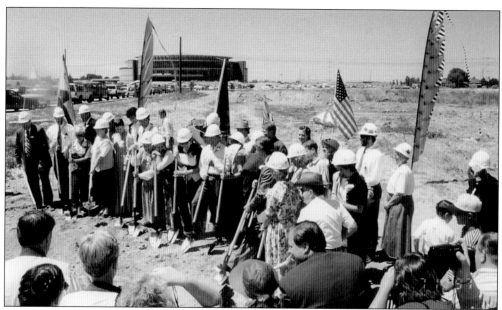

Granger-native Ruth Hale brought theater back to West Valley City when she gathered to help break ground on the new Hale Centre Theatre, just down the street from the new E-Center. On July 19, 1997, speakers included Hale family members, Mayor Gearld Wright, city manager John Patterson, and fundraising campaign chair Ned Winder (wearing a cowboy hat). (KC.)

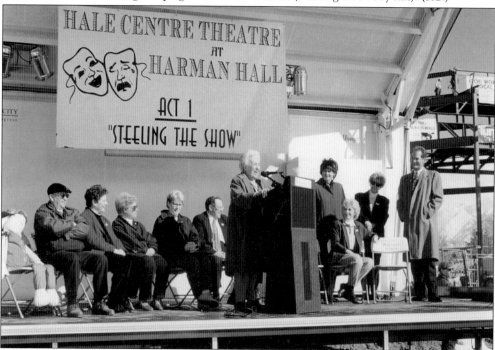

At 88 years old, Ruth Hale speaks at an event to mark a milestone in the construction of the $8.2-million theater. From left to right are city council members Russ Brook, Margaret Peterson, Janice Fisher, Barbara Thomas, Mayor Gearld Wright, Ruth Hale, Sally Dietlein, Sally Hale Rice, and Mark Dietlein. Pete Harman's secretary is seated in front of Dietlein and Rice. (KC.)

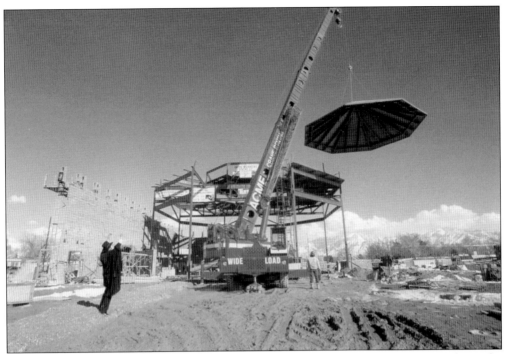

The "Phantom of the Opera" came out for a special construction event to "magically" direct the roof onto the new Hale Centre Theatre. Ruth and Nathan Hale (who died in 1994) put on their first play at the Granger Ward in 1937 (see page 29). The community had great enthusiasm for seeing this Granger-grown talent return to the area. (KC.)

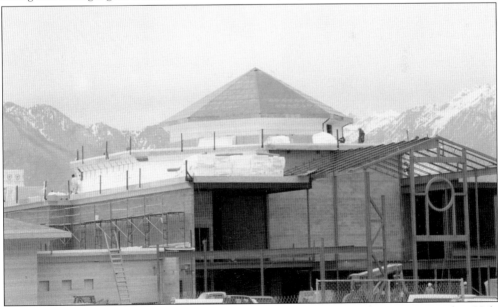

With the Wasatch Mountains in the background, construction on the 41,900-square-foot Hale Centre Theatre continues. Designed by Sizemore Floyd Architects of Atlanta, construction was handled by Turner Construction. The 520-seat theater replaced a much smaller one in South Salt Lake and was the Hale family's fourth theater, including one in Glendale, California. (KC.)

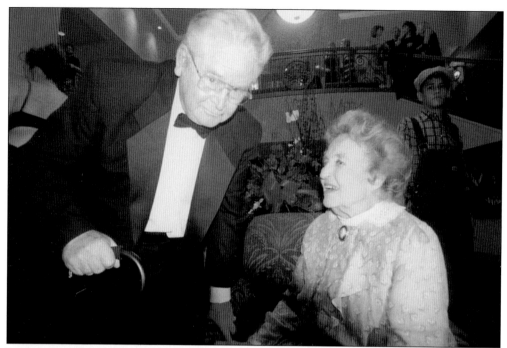

Lifelong friends Pete Harman and Ruth Hale enjoy themselves at the theater's opening. Harman was the owner of the world's first Kentucky Fried Chicken and helped fund the construction of the Hale Centre Theatre at Harman Hall, as it was formally called. In 1989, he turned his boyhood home at 4090 South 3600 West Street into the David and Grace Harman Family Home—the city's first senior center. (KC.)

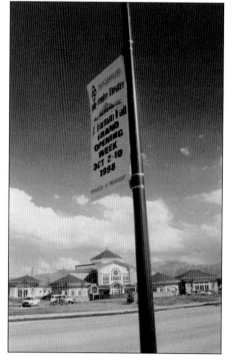

The theater's opening week was October 2–10, 1998. Hale Centre Theatre grew to bring over 250,000 patrons through its doors each year and a dedicated season ticket base of 20,500. The wide variety of dramas, comedies, and musicals at the theater are showcased on a $1 million state-of-the-art hydraulic stage. (KC.)

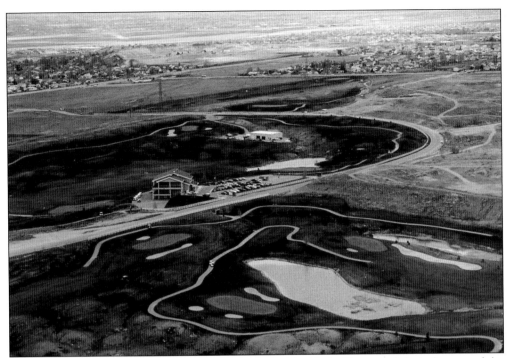

When the city annexed Hercules in 1988, it promised to build a buffer around the industry, and the West Ridge Golf Course was part of the answer. The 18-hole, Bill Neff–designed course opened in 1990 as the city's first golf course, complete with a clubhouse and breathtaking views of the entire Salt Lake Valley. This April 1997 photograph shows the golf course to the southeast. (KC.)

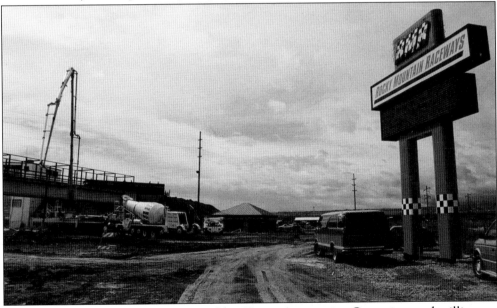

From 1996 to 1997, Spencer Young and his Young Automotive Group invested millions to upgrade the old Bonneville Raceway at 6555 West 2100 South Street. The state-of-the-art Rocky Mountain Raceways opened in March 1997. It has been popular for NASCAR-sanctioned oval and drag strip races. (KC.)

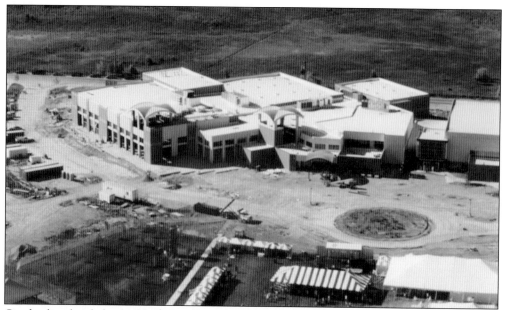

City leaders decided to build a $13-million Family Fitness Center to address the recreational needs of the community. It would include a climbing wall, two swimming pools, an indoor track, and an "edutainment" center. Located at the edge of Centennial Park (named in honor of Utah's 1996 statehood centennial), the center was built at 5415 West 3100 South Street. (KC.)

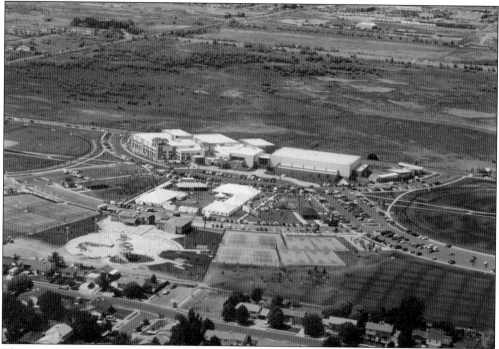

This aerial view of the Family Fitness Center shows WestFest happening in the foreground at Centennial Park, as well as the various outdoor pools, courts, and open space. Looking northwest beyond 3100 South Street is the empty area later developed as the Highbury neighborhood by the real estate arm of the LDS church. (KC.)

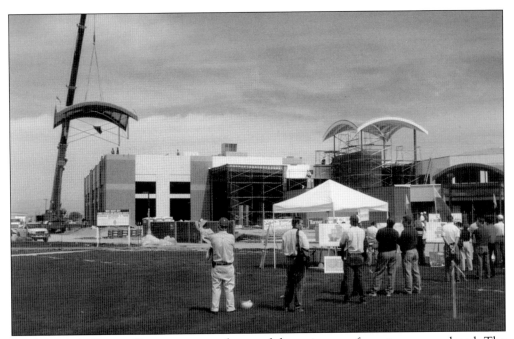

As the Family Fitness Center progressed, one of the unique roof capstones was placed. The 96,000-square-foot facility included the state's tallest indoor waterslide, a children's splash area, basketball and racquetball courts, cardio equipment, and dance and aerobic rooms. It would also have community rooms and meeting space on the second story. (KC.)

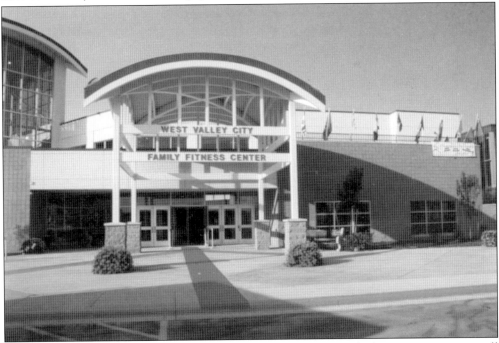

The Family Fitness Center opened on October 1, 1999. In general, the center was very well received by the community. Many were thrilled to have the state's newest and finest recreation center nearby. It received a 2010 Nickelodeon Parent's Choice Award. (KC.)

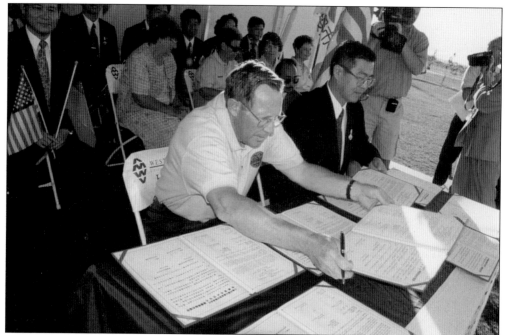

In 1999, the city formed its first sister city relationship with Nantou, Taiwan—a city in a mountain valley with a similar population size. Mayor Gearld Wright led a delegation of city leaders to Taiwan in 1999, and in 2000, Nantou mayor Zhao-Qing Lee came to West Valley City to sign the documents formalizing the relationship. Police sergeant Terry Chen (shown between the mayors) helped immensely with the relationship. (KC.)

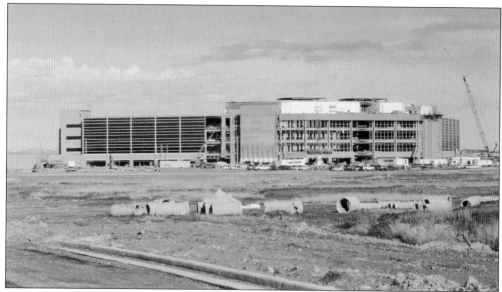

Utah's largest business park was created in West Valley City when the real estate arm of the LDS church developed the Lake Park Corporate Center west of Bangerter Highway at the city's northern entrance. Stonebridge, a 27-hole, Johnny Miller–designed golf course, helped provide green space. Discover Financial completed this 410,000-square-foot building in 1998. The company became the city's largest employer when it created 3,000 jobs. (KC.)

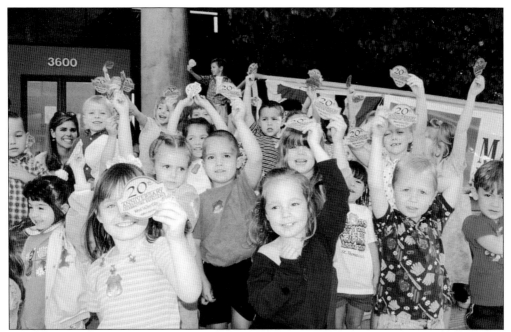

In 2000, West Valley City celebrated 20 years of incorporation. Young people who came through city hall on Maryl McKnight Youth Pride Day could earn a special 20th anniversary patch by visiting each city department and learning their function. These young people from Miss Margene's Preschool proudly display their patch. (KC.)

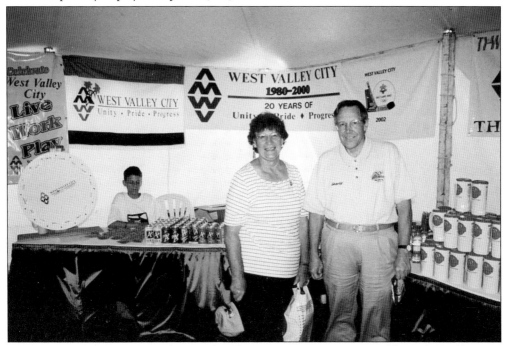

Justin Anfinsen volunteers in the city's booth at WestFest as Mayor Gearld Wright and his wife Lila stop by for a visit. The city was not only celebrating its 20th anniversary in 2000, it was looking forward to being a venue city for the 2002 Winter Olympic Games. (KC.)

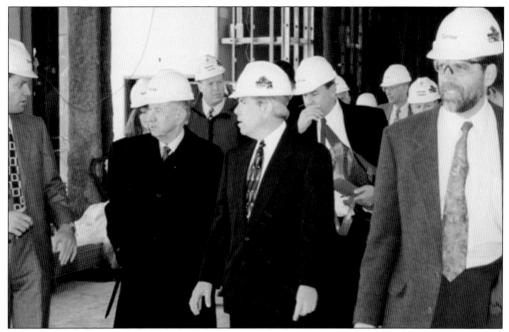

During the preparations for the Olympics, city manager John Patterson gives International Olympic Committee president Juan Antonio Samaranch a tour of the E-Center. Salt Lake Organizing Committee president Tom Welch is standing behind Patterson. To the far right is Jim Cost of Turner Construction. (KC.)

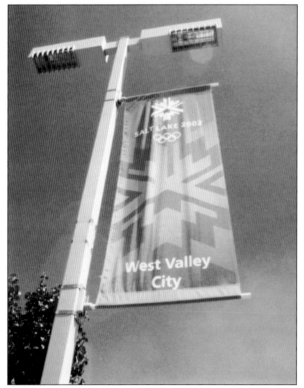

Banners were posted on city streets as the Olympics neared, and city-planning staff worked with businesses and homes along major traffic corridors to spruce up and improve their appearances to welcome the world. Retiring police chief Dennis Nordfelt was named city Olympic coordinator, and plans were in full swing for the Games. (KC.)

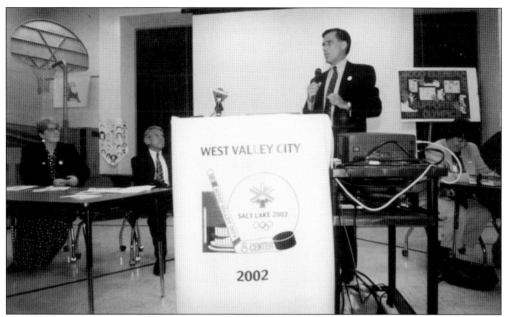

As the Olympics approached, stakeholder meetings were held to discuss the impact of the Games and the logistics of hosting them. At this meeting, held at Redwood Elementary School, Salt Lake Organizing Committee president Mitt Romney addresses the group. From left to right are council member Barbara Thomas, city manager John Patterson, Romney, and council member Carolynn Burt. (KC.)

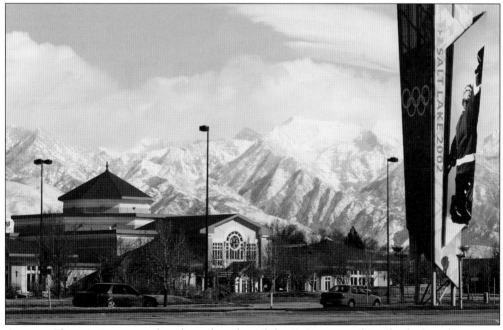

A giant Olympic icon was placed on the edge of the E-Center parking lot before the games, welcoming the world to the ice hockey venue. The Hale Centre Theatre, east across Decker Lake Drive, hosted the National Hockey League's Stanley Cup as a special exhibit during the Games. The NHL rented the facility for the two-week period. (Jeffrey Allred, DN.)

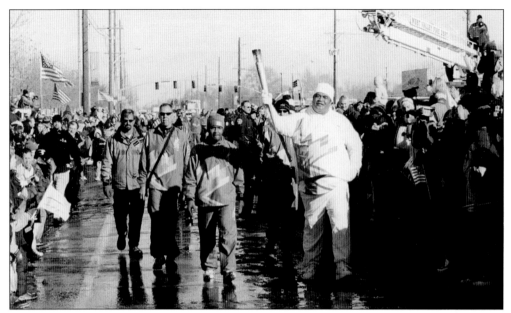

On February 8, 2002, at 8:30 a.m., the Olympic flame arrived in West Valley City at Redwood Road. The torch turned west at 3100 South Street, then south at 4000 West Street. At 9:30 a.m., the relay turned onto 3500 South Street and headed east. At 2700 West Street, the torch turned south toward city hall (where this photograph was taken). (KC.)

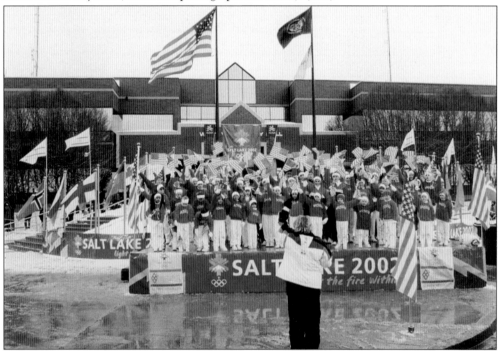

At city hall, a crowd gathered to greet the torch runners and was entertained by Miss Margene's Creative Generation Musical Theater, conducted by Margene Conde. At 9:45 a.m., the Olympic torch arrived to the celebration at city hall. After a brief pause, the torch went east on 3800 South Street to Redwood Road and then south to Taylorsville. The flame left the city at 10:15 a.m. (KC.)

City hall was ready for the Winter Games! The city saw ice hockey at the E-Center. Heineken rented the city's clubhouse at West Ridge Golf Course for the official Dutch "house." The city was also paired with Canada as part of an adopt-a-team program, and several activities with athletes were held. (KC.)

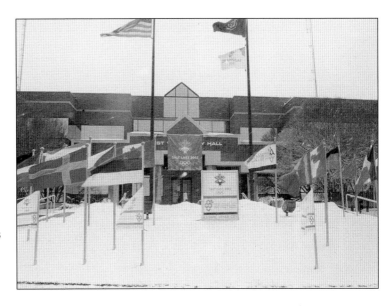

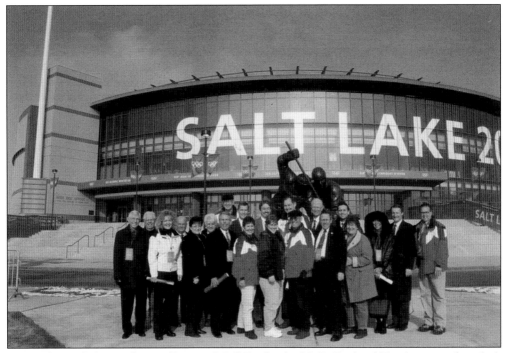

Pictured from left to right are (first row) Bill England of C.R. England Trucking; unidentified; executive assistant Cindy Johnson; human resources manager Paul Isaac; recorder Sheri McKendrick; Glenda Nordfelt; city manager John Patterson; council members Carolynn Burt, Barbara Thomas, and Russ Brooks; Mayor Gearld Wright; Lila Wright; media relations director Tammy Kikuchi; finance director Jim Welch; and event manager Kevin Conde; (second row) Olympic coordinator Dennis Nordfelt; parks director Kevin Astill; attorney Richard Catten; public works director Russ Willardson; community and economic development director Joseph Moore; and assistant city manager Wayne Pyle. (WVCHS.)

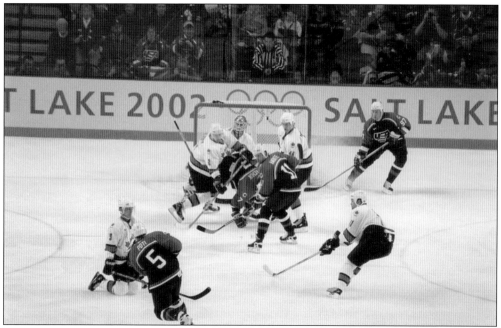

The E-Center was the primary ice hockey venue for the Games and saw 14 men's teams and 8 women's teams play (the Peaks Ice Arena in Provo also had some preliminary round games). A particularly exciting game was when Team USA beat Russia on the day of the 22-year anniversary of the "Miracle on Ice" game of 1980. (KC.)

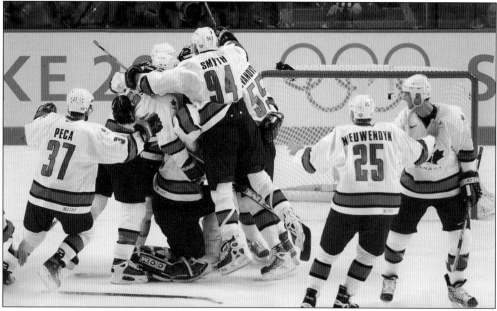

On February 24, 2002, Canada celebrated winning the Olympic gold medal with a score of 5-2 over the US silver medalists. Russia won the bronze. On the women's side, Canada also won the gold, United States the silver, and Sweden the bronze. The legend of the "Lucky Loonie" was born when Canadian ice-maker Trent Evans admitted to burying a Canadian $1 coin or Loonie under the E-Center's center ice. (Photograph by Ravell Call; courtesy DN.)

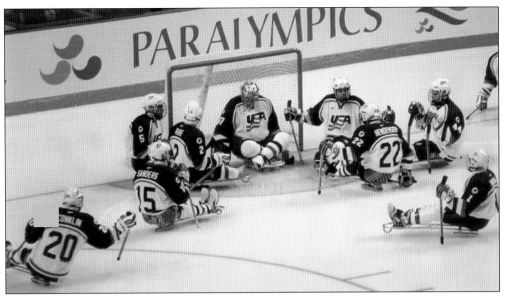

The Paralympic Winter Games were held March 7–16, 2012, and West Valley City's E-Center was host to the sledge hockey events. Six nations competed, and despite being seeded sixth, Team USA went on to win the gold medal by defeating Norway in a thrilling game in an overtime shootout. Sweden had defeated Canada to win the bronze. (KC.)

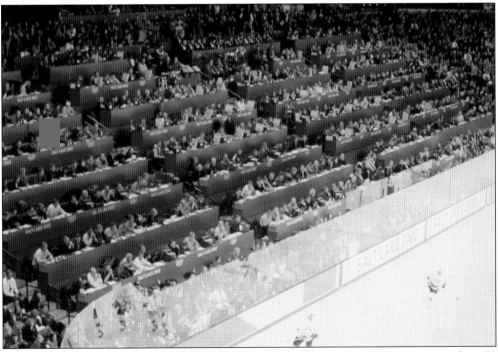

The world media gathered in West Valley City during the Olympics, including reporters from 78 nations and six continents. The much-anticipated final matchup between the United States and Canada resulted in the highest television ratings in Olympic history up to that time. In the United States, the gold-medal game was the most watched hockey game, Olympic or NHL, since the 1980 Winter Olympics. In Canada, the game was the most-watched sports program ever. (KC.)

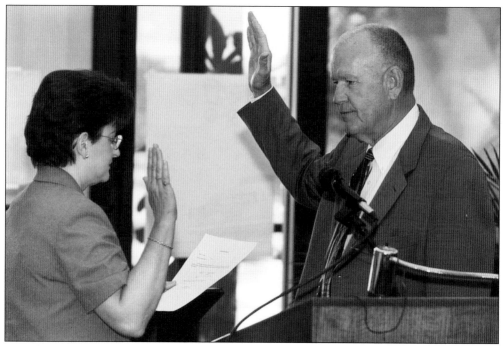

On July 25, 2002, just a few months into an unprecedented third term, Mayor Gearld Wright died suddenly from a massive stroke. The city council decided to appoint Dennis Nordfelt as the city's sixth mayor. Nordfelt had served as city police chief from 1987 to 1998 and had just retired as city Olympic coordinator. City recorder Sheri McKendrick swore him in on August 20, 2002. (Photograph by Michael Brandy, courtesy DN.)

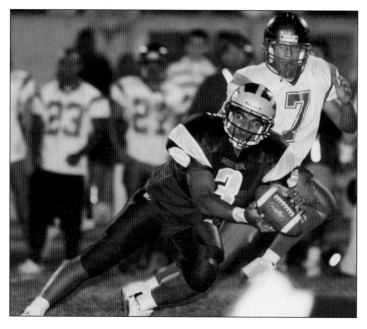

A rivalry game between the city's two high schools took place on September 25, 2002, when the Hunter Wolverines met the Granger Lancers. The Wolverines were still smarting from the 28-point loss to the Lancers in 2001 and pushed hard for a 21-14 victory that night. Hunter High's Tauni Vakapuna is seen making a catch despite being covered by Granger High's Lance Correa. (Photograph by Chuck Wing, courtesy DN.)

Seven

UNITY, PRIDE, PROGRESS
2003–2011

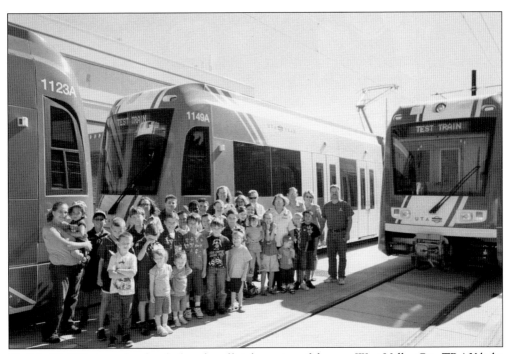

On July 15, 2011, just a few days before the official opening of the new West Valley City TRAX light rail line, Utah Transit Authority board member Necia Christensen takes her neighborhood Cub Scout pack for a test ride. Among the group was her husband, council member Don Christensen, and the city's first lady, Karyn Winder. TRAX was a significant milestone for a continuously progressing West Valley City. (KC.)

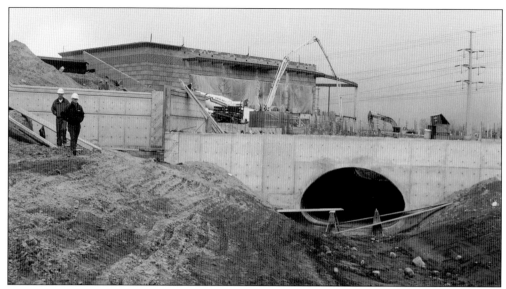

Project engineer Brian McBeth (left) of Layton Construction and city economic development administrator Bob Buchanan look over construction of the city's new Utah Cultural Celebration Center on March 27, 2003. The first phase of the 27-acre site at 1355 West 3100 South Street included the main building, an outdoor amphitheater, and a large festival area. (Jason Olson, DN.)

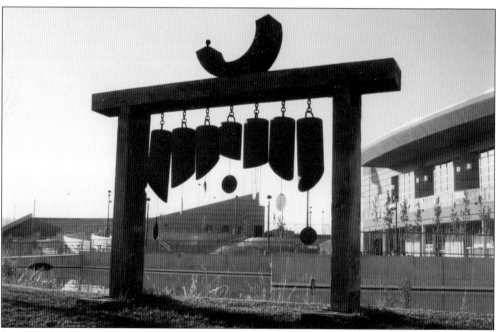

In 2003, the West Valley City Arts Council commissioned local artist Chris Coleman to make three sets of bells, which was the first public art gift to the new Utah Cultural Celebration Center. The bells are contemporary works made from recycled compressed air tanks. On windy days, their chimes can be heard as far away as Redwood Road. (KC.)

In May 2004, a six-ton, seven-foot-tall replica of an ancient Olmec head was donated to the Utah Cultural Celebration Center by the Mexican state of Veracruz. The head, which is on permanent display at the center, is one of only three in the United States—the others being at the Chicago Field Museum and the Smithsonian in Washington, DC. (KC.)

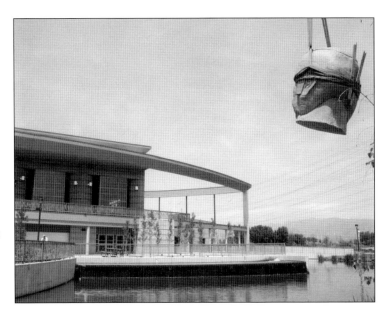

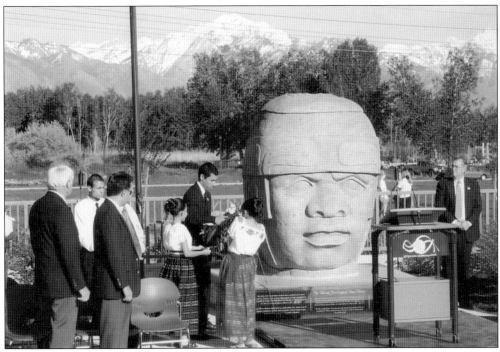

Unveiled to the public on May 22, 2004, the arrival of the Olmec head marked the beginning of West Valley City's second sister city relationship with Boca del Rio in the Mexican state of Veracruz. Staff members are on either side of the head preparing for the sister city ceremony. Adan Carillo is to the left of the head, and Kevin Conde is to the right. (WVCHS.)

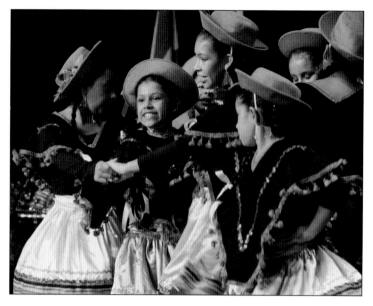

Members of Fantasy and Folklore perform during the 2008 International Summer Festival and Education Fair at the Utah Cultural Celebration Center on Saturday, August 9, 2008. West Valley City had grown into Utah's most ethnically diverse city, with 45 percent ethnic minorities. The UCCC became a place to celebrate the positives of diversity. (Photograph by Ashley Lowery; courtesy DN.)

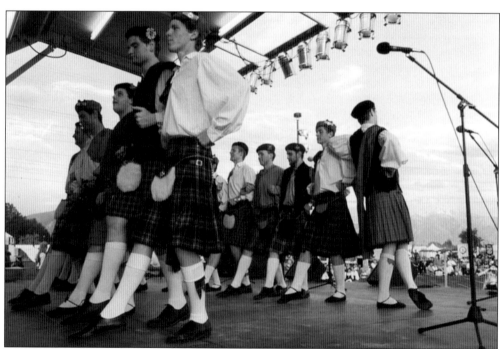

The West Jordan Theater Arts group performs on the first day of the Utah Scottish Festival and Highland Games held at the Utah Cultural Celebration Center on Friday, June 13, 2003. Groups representing the cultures of a variety of European, Latin American, Asian, and African nations have come to the center for their festivals. (Photograph by Kira Horvath; courtesy DN.)

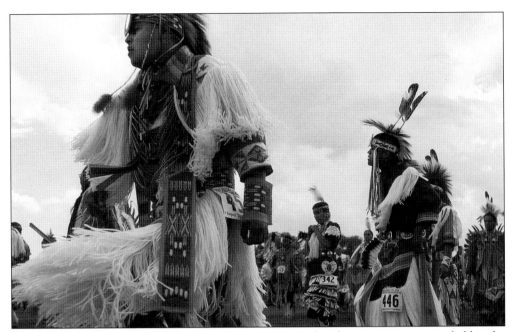

The fifth annual West Valley City Native American Festival and contest powwow was held at the Utah Cultural Celebration Center August 22–24, 2003. Here, Jason Nakai dances during the grand entry on August 23. Harry James of the Navajo Nation and his wife, Prestine James, formed the Native American Association of West Valley in 1997. (Photograph by Kira Horvath; courtesy DN.)

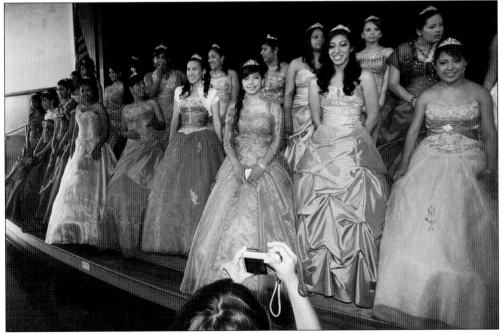

At the Madre e Hija Expo, 44 *quinceaneras* pose for photographs. Sponsored by *El Observador* of Utah, the grand gala was held at the Utah Cultural Celebration Center on Saturday, May 28, 2011. The Hispanic population of the city grew rapidly and made up one-third of city residents in the 2010 census. (Photograph by Brian Nicholson; courtesy DN.)

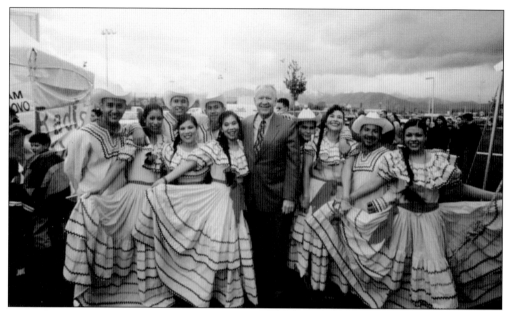

At a Cinco de Mayo event sponsored by Telemundo, Mayor Dennis Nordfelt poses with entertainers at the city's Centennial Park at 5405 West 3100 South Street. The 2010 census showed that 31 percent of West Valley City residents spoke a language other than English at home, with Spanish being the largest of that group. The city launched an English language initiative in January 2011 to encourage a common tongue. (KC.)

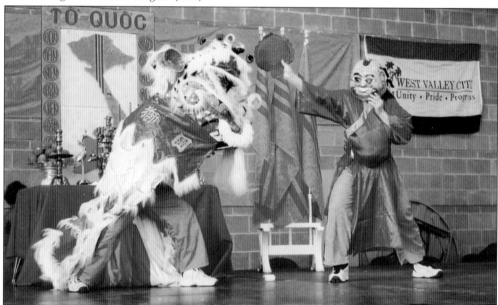

A lion dance is performed as part of a Vietnamese New Year celebration held at the Utah Cultural Celebration Center. The 2010 census showed that five percent of city residents were Asian. Vietnamese residents made up the largest subgroup within that category. Vietnamese businesses have flourished on 3500 South Street and on Redwood Road. In November 2011, Tom Huynh, a Vietnamese American, was elected as the city's first minority council member. (Courtesy Michael Christensen.)

The city's Utah Cultural Celebration Center has attracted notable visitors, such as on May 23, 2006, when Mexican president Vicente Fox and Marta Sahagun de Fox visited. They wave to dancers from Midvale Elementary with Utah attorney general Mark Shurtleff sitting at President Fox's left. Fox came to Utah as part of a three-state swing that included visits to Washington and California. (Photograph by Scott Winterton; courtesy DN.)

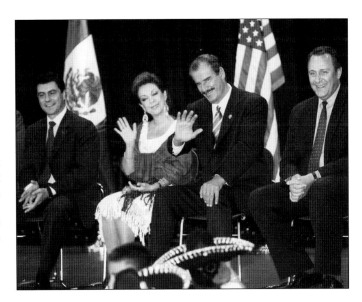

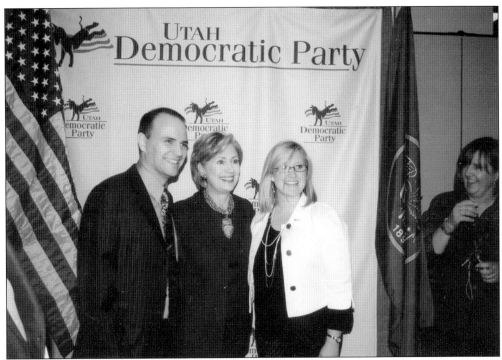

At the invitation of council member Corey Rushton, New York senator and former first lady Hillary Rodham Clinton visited the Utah Cultural Celebration Center stumping for presidential candidate Sen. Barack Obama (D-IL). From left to right are Corey Rushton, Clinton, Rushton's wife, Emily Rushton, and Karen Hale. Hale and Emily Rushton were delegates to the Democratic National Convention. The visit took place on October 25, 2008. (KC.)

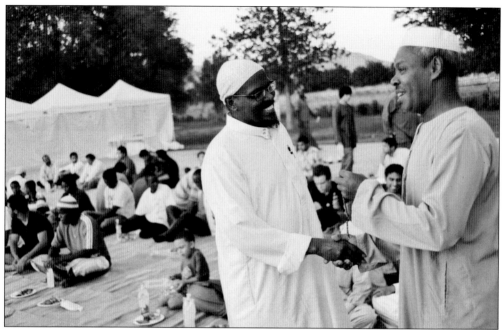

Mohamed Magtoof (right) and Ali Yussuf greet each other at Khadeeja Mosque for the start of Ramadan on Saturday, August 14, 2010. Three mosques in Utah serve up to 20,000 Muslims, but the Khadeeja Mosque at 1070 West 2350 South Street in West Valley City is by far the state's largest. (Photograph by Matt Gillis; courtesy DN.)

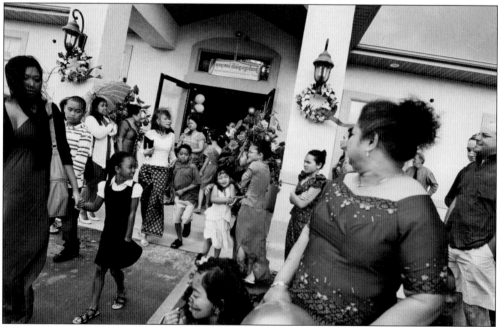

Congregants and friends gather out front of the Cambodian Christian Reformed Church at 4035 South 5600 West Street for the dedication ceremony on Sunday, June 19, 2011. West Valley City represents many diverse faiths, including a Buddhist Temple, a Tongan United Methodist Church, and a Jehovah's Witness Kingdom Hall. (Photograph by Mike Terry; courtesy DN.)

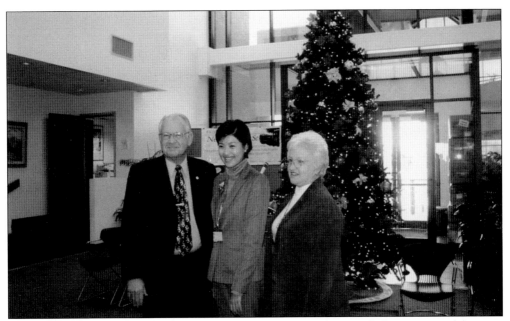

During December 2005 the newly elected mayor of Nantou, Taiwan, led a sister city delegation to West Valley City. From left to right are Mayor Dennis Nordfelt, Mayor Shu-Hua Hsu, and First Lady Glenda Nordfelt. West Valley City businesses sent masks to Nantou during the SARS outbreak of 2003, and Nantou leaders have shared their lessons learned from a 7.3 earthquake with West Valley City officials. (KC.)

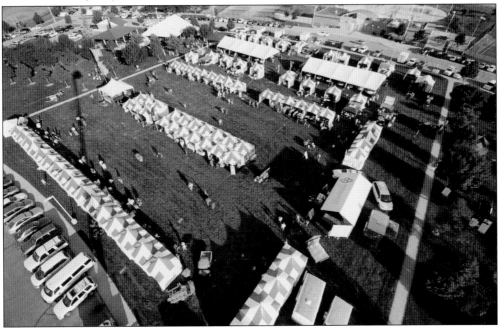

As seen in this 2008 aerial photograph, the summer tradition of WestFest continued in its new location at Centennial Park. The city's "showmobile" portable stage is seen on the right. The outdoor swimming pool and waterslide of Centennial Park are visible in the distance. For several years, helicopter rides allowed residents to enjoy views such as this one. (KC.)

113

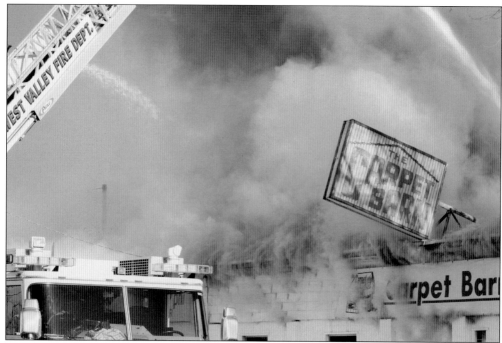

On December 31, 2009, the Carpet Barn went up in flames and West Valley City firefighters battled to contain the inferno. An employee who was using a weed burner to melt ice on the loading dock started the fire at the 42-year-old business at 3725 South Redwood Road. (KC.)

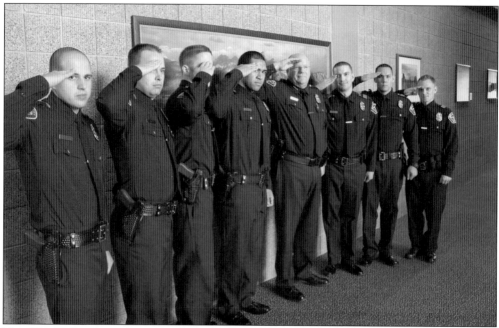

New West Valley City police officers salute after their post-graduation event on April 22, 2011. From left to right are officers Lloyd, Fox, Fife, and Aulai, police chief Thayle "Buzz" Nielsen, and officers Ben Christensen, Chow, and Clegg. City police helped direct an overall reduction of crime in the city starting in 2006 and are recognized for stellar police work on critical investigations. (KC.)

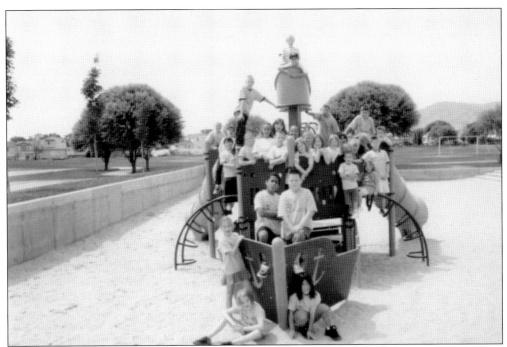

Family Fitness Center Day Camp participants pause on the playground of Centennial Park. In 2010, in addition to the Family Fitness Center, the city had 22 parks, a growing network of trails, the Harman Senior Recreation Center, and the Stonebridge and West Ridge golf courses. (KC.)

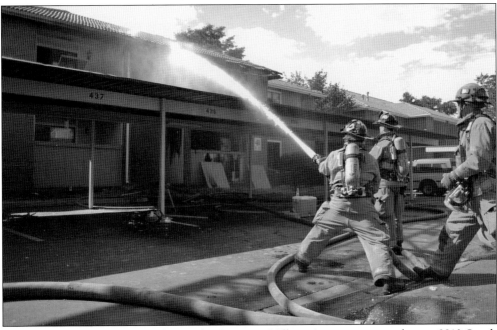

Firefighters work to put out a fire at the Somerset Village Apartment complex on 3810 South Redwood Road. The two-alarm blaze of Tuesday, July 20, 2010, destroyed two units and displaced eight families. West Valley City firefighters were able to contain the fire, which started on one of the unit's balconies. (Photograph by Matt Gillis; courtesy DN.)

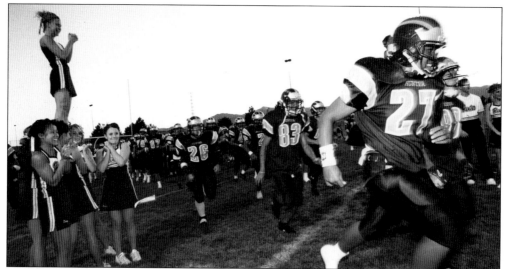

Despite a winless first season in 1990, Hunter High School typically had a strong football program, including winning the state championship in 2003. The excitement continued on Friday, October 14, 2005, when the Hunter Wolverines ran onto the field for their matchup with the Kearns Cougars. They won the game 48-10. (Photograph by Brian Nicholson; courtesy DN.)

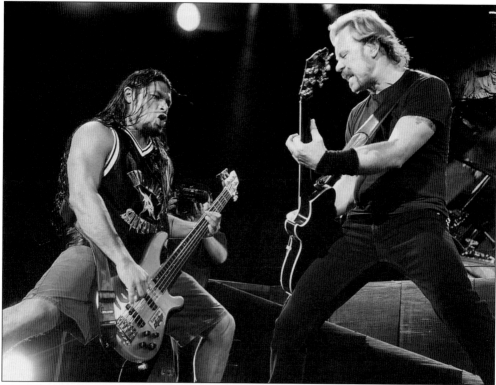

The USANA Amphitheatre opened in 2003 just west of the West Ridge Golf Course. With 20,000 seats and outdoor seating, the venue attracts top summer concerts. Metallica stopped by to rock out on August 6, 2003. After the show, band members spent more than $200 at the Burger King on 5600 West Street. (DN.)

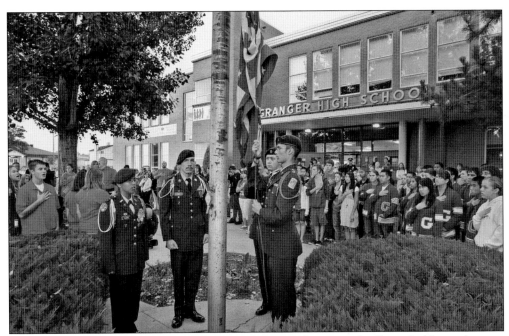

On Thursday morning, September 11, 2008, ROTC members raise the flag to half-mast during a 9/11-commemoration ceremony in front of Granger High School. Granger's student body officers are on the right and hundreds of students came out to commemorate the tragic event that happened when the high school students were in grade school. (Tom Smart, DN)

The cross-town rivalry between Granger High School and Hunter High School continued in women's sports, as well. This match between the two schools was held on November 4, 2003. As of 2011, the enrollment at Hunter High was 2,100, while 1,500 attended Granger High. About one-third of students at Cyprus High in Magna came from West Valley City, as did many students at Taylorsville High. (Jeffrey Allred, DN.)

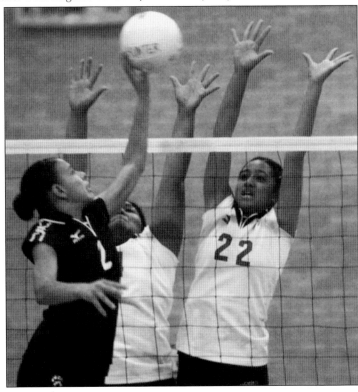

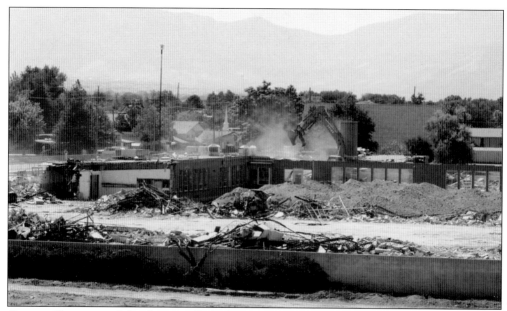

Granger Elementary School, originally built at 2450 West 3800 South Street, was torn down in 2006. In a three-way deal, West Valley City provided property at 3700 South 1950 West Street for a new Granger Elementary, the Granite School District invested in building the new school, and Costco (built at the former site of the school) donated a computer lab to compensate for the inconvenience. (KC.)

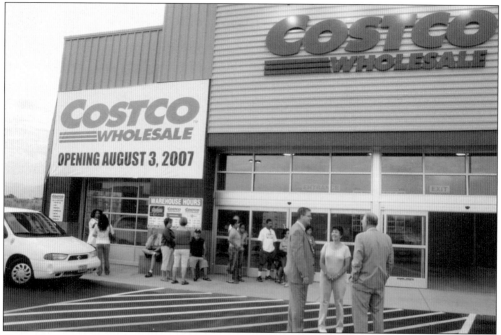

Council member Joel Coleman converses with city council colleague Carolynn Burt and Mayor Dennis Nordfelt at the grand opening of the city's new Costco Wholesale Warehouse on August 3, 2007. The new facility helped buoy the city's tax base and marked the first step in the redevelopment of the Valley Fair Mall area. (KC.)

In May 2006, eight Boy Scouts of West Valley Troop 677 received their Eagle Scout Award. From left to right are Cory Mortensen, Joel Whitmer, Ivan Clark, Newton Carlicci, Isaac MacFarlane, Trevor Blair, Robin Clark, and Derrick Carter. Many young men in the city continue to be involved with the Scouting program. (Tiffany De Masters, DN.)

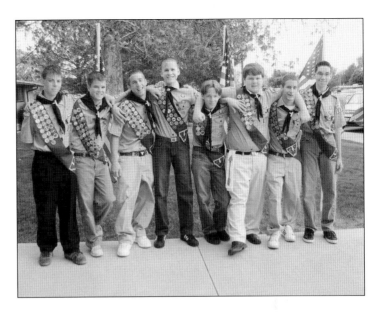

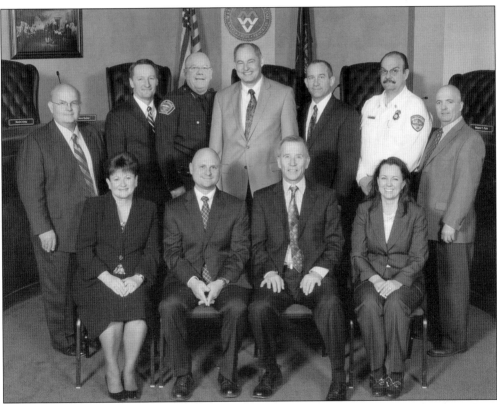

The city executive staff members in January 2012 are, from left to right, (first row) recorder Sheri McKendrick, attorney Eric Bunderson, parks director Kevin Astill, and community and economic development director Nicole Cottle; (second row) assistant city manager Paul Isaac, finance director Jim Welch, police chief Buzz Nielsen, public works director Russ Willardson, city manager Wayne Pyle, fire chief John Evans, and community preservation director Layne Morris. (WVCHS.)

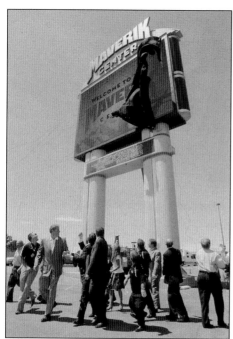

On Saturday, July 10, 2010, representatives from West Valley City, Maverik, and the arena management pulled off the cover of the main marquee, unveiling the new name—the Maverik Center. After 13 years of searching for the right fit, officials were thrilled to develop a partnership with Maverik, a chain of convenience stores with an adventure theme. (Photograph by Scott Winterton; courtesy DN.)

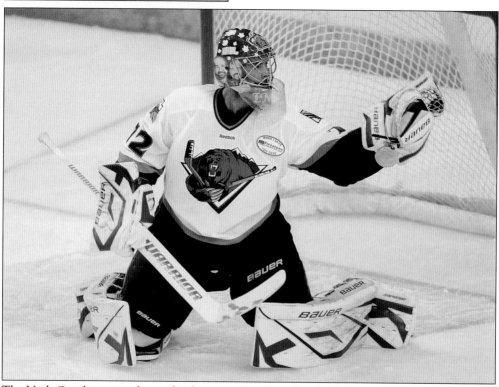

The Utah Grizzlies minor league hockey team has played in the E-Center, now Maverik Center, since the building opened. Grizzlies goalkeeper (No. 72) Andrew Engelage makes a great save as the Grizzlies play the Idaho Steelheads in the season opener on Friday, October 14, 2011. (Photograph by Scott Winterton; courtesy DN.)

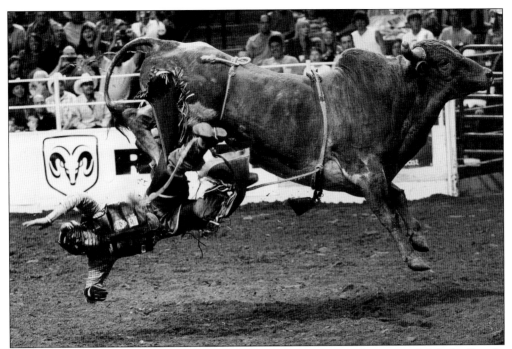

In recent years, the Days of '47 Rodeo was held at the Salt Palace in downtown Salt Lake City, In 2009, the rodeo was successfully brought to West Valley City. Riker Carter of Stone, Idaho, gets thrown from his ride in the bull-riding competition during the Days of '47 Rodeo at the Maverik Center on Monday, July 25, 2011. (Photograph by Brian Nicholson; courtesy DN.)

Participants appreciated the convenience and quality facility of the Maverik Center for the Days of '47 Rodeo. Here, Lindsay Sears from Nanton, Alberta, Canada, competes in the barrel-racing competition during the Days of '47 Rodeo on July 25, 2011. The rodeo, celebrating the Mormon pioneers coming to Utah in 1847, has been held continuously each year since 1849. (Photograph by Brian Nicholson; courtesy DN.)

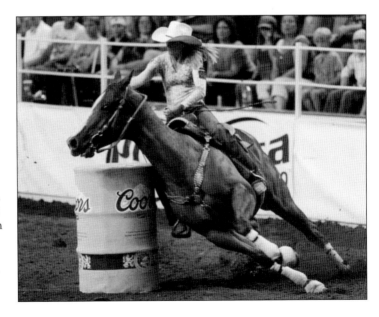

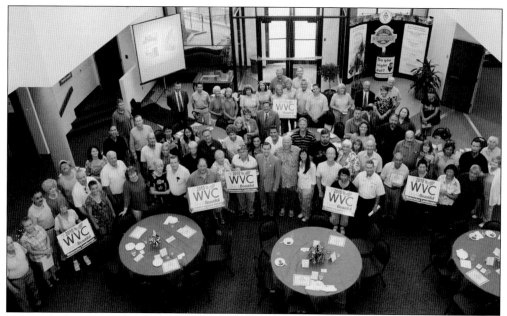

The city's Clean and Beautiful Committee recognizes approximately 75 residences and businesses each year that look exceptional. Award recipients are given a yard sign to display in front of their home or business and are recognized at an awards reception before a city council meeting. This photograph shows 2011 winners with Mayor Mike Winder and the city council at the spring 2011 reception in the lobby of city hall. (KC.)

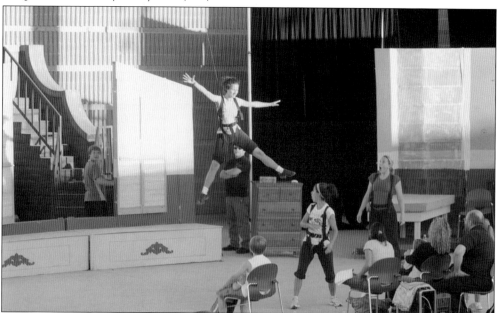

Peter Pan was the city's 2010 Arts Council production. Performed at the outdoor amphitheater at the Utah Cultural Celebration Center, it starred twins Jamie and Melissa Jackson (one as Peter Pan and one in flight as Peter's shadow). Tracee Conde Walker, who played Wendy, looks on open-mouthed in the rehearsal. Directed by Jim Smith and choreographed by Margene Conde, 60 people participated in the production. (KC.)

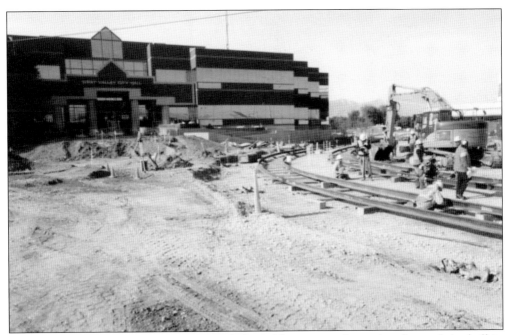

Construction on the West Valley TRAX light rail line moves forward in front of city hall in 2010. The 5.1 mile extension came at a cost of $370 million, but it was completed a year ahead of schedule and 20 percent under budget. Numerous meetings were held between city leaders and Utah Transit Authority over the years that the line was planned and built. (KC.)

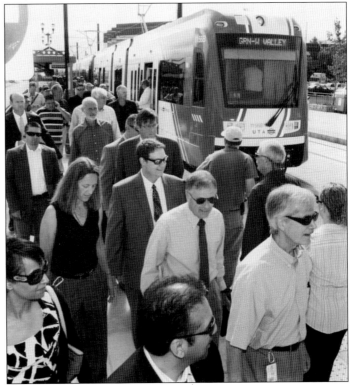

Ceremonies to launch the new West Valley and Mid-Jordan TRAX extensions were held on August 2, 2011. State and local leaders and transportation officials exit the train in West Valley City after riding the new lines. The West Valley extension became part of the Green Line that takes passengers downtown and eventually to the Salt Lake International Airport. Regular service began on August 7. (Photograph by Ravell Call; courtesy DN.)

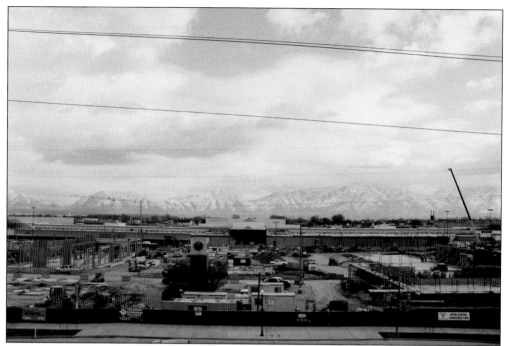

In 2010, the Valley Fair Mall was in the midst of its biggest renovation since it first opened in 1970. This view from atop city hall shows new buildings in the former parking lot taking shape to the east and construction already beginning on the new entrance. The 600,000-square-foot shopping center grew to over one million square feet. (KC.)

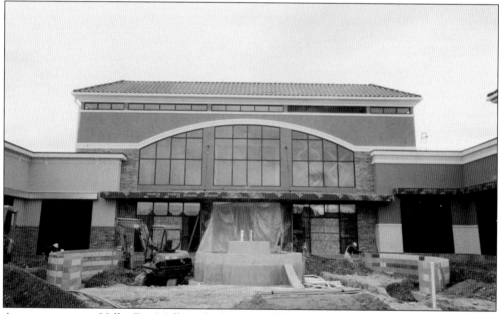

A new entrance to Valley Fair Mall was built as part of the major renovation. The grand entryway leading up to the mall would include an interactive fountain with 31 jets, some reaching as high as 30 feet. The fountain has LED lights in each water stream and is combined with music to create a choreographed show on the colorful splash pad. (KC.)

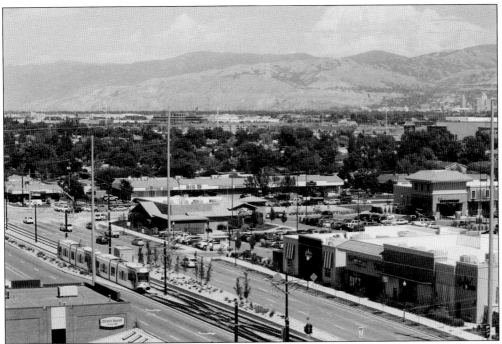

This August 2011 photograph taken from the roof of city hall shows one of the new TRAX trains arriving to the northeast. Some of the new parts of the Valley Fair Mall area are visible in the photograph. In the center of the image, on the southeast corner of 3500 South and 2700 West Streets, is the new Olive Garden, which was named the number-one restaurant of the chain in North America in 2011. (KC.)

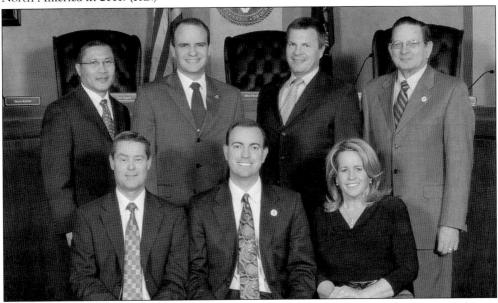

City council members in 2012 included, from left to right, (first row) Steve Vincent, elected 2001; Mayor Mike Winder, elected council 2005 and mayor 2009; and Karen Lang, elected 2011; (second row) Tom Huynh, elected 2011; Mayor Pro Tem Corey Rushton, 2007; Steve Buhler, elected 2009; and Don Christensen, elected 2009. (WVCHS.)

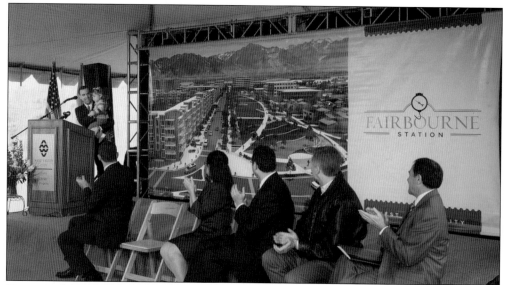

On a rainy May 19, 2011, city leaders unveiled an ambitious plan for a half-billion-dollar mixed-use development to be built west of city hall. Called "Fairbourne Station" (see page 11 for historical context), it would include a new park promenade, residential towers, and an Embassy Suites hotel. Mayor Mike Winder and three-year-old daughter Grace pushed the button to unveil the city's vision of the future. (WVC.)

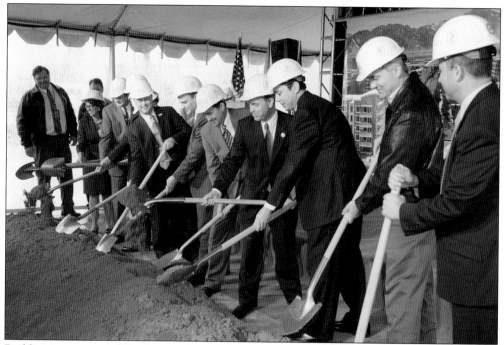

Building inspectors Jeff Pankow and Troy Glines look on as officials break ground on Fairbourne Station on May 19, 2011. From left to right are community and economic development director Nicole Cottle, council members Don Christensen, Steve Buhler, Russ Brooks, Steve Vincent, Corey Rushton, Utah governor Gary Herbert, Mayor Mike Winder, Congressman Jason Chaffetz, Congressman Jim Matheson, and city manager Wayne Pyle. (WVC.)

The new Granger High School is under construction in this October 2011 photograph. Bangerter Highway runs to the west of the school. The Oquirrh Mountains are to the southwest. The new school is being built on the old Granger Park and will be Utah's largest high school when completed, with a 2,600-student capacity. (KC.)

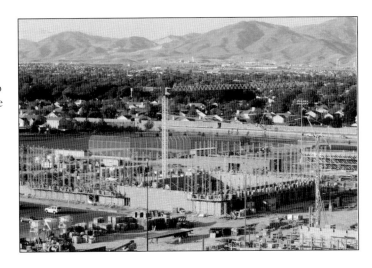

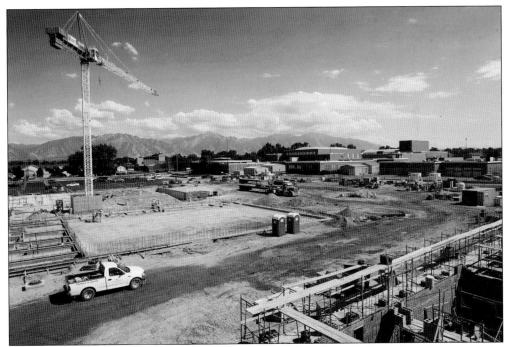

On September 13, 2011, the old school is visible to the southeast behind the construction site of the new Granger High School. The old school will be demolished once the new school is completed in 2013. The new high school, combined with Fairbourne Station to the east and the remodeled Valley Fair Mall, is part of a bold new future for West Valley City. (Photograph by Mike Terry; courtesy DN.)

DISCOVER THOUSANDS OF LOCAL HISTORY BOOKS FEATURING MILLIONS OF VINTAGE IMAGES

Arcadia Publishing, the leading local history publisher in the United States, is committed to making history accessible and meaningful through publishing books that celebrate and preserve the heritage of America's people and places.

Find more books like this at
www.arcadiapublishing.com

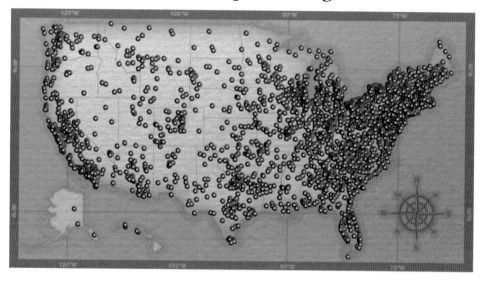

Search for your hometown history, your old stomping grounds, and even your favorite sports team.

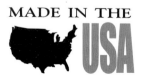